I0007170

The Digital
CURRENCY REVOLUTION

Sebastian Schulze

Contre l'ancien régime
~~Burn the Banks!~~ -> Join the Currency Revolution!
~~Millionaire by Christmas!~~ -> Change the world!

Why and How to invest and trade with
Ripple (or Stellar) in Bitcoin and
other currencies, valuables, shares, contracts,
natural resources, ideas, ...

License notes

This is Book 1 of the Financial Independence Basics (series)
by caveat emptor publishers.

This is the early preview Create Space edition
2014-11-21 (without pictures and graphs) by caveat emptor
publishers.

caveat (™) emptor

Part of the match book program. That means if you ordered the
paperback (at CreateSpace) the e-book (Kindle) is for free.

Sebastian Schulze

The CreateSpace ID 5061049.
www.createspace.com/5061049

ISBN-13: 978-1502910424

ISBN-10: 150291042X

KDP edition ASIN: B00PYDUCF6

www.amazon.com/dp/B00PYDUCF6

The author accepts no responsibility or liability for content that is provided under external links.

Caveat emptor publishers / Financial Independence Basics are an imprint / brand of the author.

If you have questions or any suggestion for improvement please contact the author at: **euauthor@gmail.com**

Disclaimer

As the Bitstamp exchange's risk warning is putting it[1]:

"The trading of goods and products, real or virtual, as well as virtual currencies involves significant risk. Prices can and do fluctuate on any given day. Due to such price fluctuations, you may increase or lose value in your assets at any given moment. Any currency - virtual or not - may be subject to large swings in value and may even become worthless. There is an inherent risk that losses will occur as a result of buying, selling or trading anything on a market.

Bitcoin trading also has special risks not generally shared with official currencies or goods or commodities in a market. Unlike most currencies, which are backed by governments or other legal entities, or by commodities such as gold or silver, Bitcoin is a unique kind of "fiat" currency, backed by technology and trust. There is no central bank that can take corrective measure to protect the value of Bitcoins in a crisis or issue more currency."

All content provided in this book is for information purposes only. Do your own due diligence before investing in anything.

This author is not offering any services or financial tools described in this book. I am not affiliated with any exchange or currency creator. I am not presenting myself as a registered investment advisor or broker dealer.

Trading in the financial and currency market involves high risk of possible complete loss of investment. Do not trade with or invest money you cannot afford to lose. Losses might occur in a very short period of time. Investing in and trading with any digital currency entails risk including but not limited to changing political or economic conditions that may substantially affect the price or

---

[1] [https://www.bitstamp.net/risk-warning/]

liquidity of exchanges, markets, etc. There is a chance that digital currencies might be outlawed by governments or fail and disappear "overnight".

Before deciding to participate in a market carefully consider your objectives, level of experience and the risk involved. Digital currencies (currently) entail limited regulatory protection and a high market volatility.

When investing you are advised to factor in the possibility that you could sustain a total loss of all your funds. I do not guarantee that readers acting upon any suggestion mentioned or discussed will anyhow profit financially.

All decisions to act or not to act upon any suggestions or information given in this book is the sole responsibility of the reader. I strongly implore you to consult other literature and experts and so get a third opinion before making any kind of investment decision.

I will not be held responsible or liable to readers or any other parties for losses that may be sustained from reading this book and trying to invest and trade with the described methods in the described currencies or other assets.

Especially be aware that in sending money and other assets through block chain based currencies and protocols in most cases there is no way to get your money back (no refund, charge back, etc.) if the address the money was sent to was wrong or proves untrustworthy.

"The subprime crisis revealed a simple fact, that is, **that finance is nothing but a fraud** [...] fraud **in terms of arbitrage**, a trading strategy seeking to profit from a difference in the prices of an asset in two different markets: "As it has turned out, finance was the **arbitrage of knowledge gaps** between **those who know** [those in the financial industry] and **those who don't** [the public], **not arbitrage between markets**, and this fact has been revealed." [...] financial market insiders [...] had known this all along, but now that the **fraudulent nature of finance** had been disclosed, [...] **no further innovation in financial technologies would be possible.**"[2]
Hirokazu Miyazaki citing a senior securities trader

Or something like that was the assumption that the **general public and politicians alike had learned from the damage of the crises**. Perhaps it was to be expected, that the financial sector would have to deal with **more stringent legal requirements** relating to complex financial products and manipulations. Such **assumptions and hypothesis naturally proved foolish**, nearly 6 years later **everything seems to be 'back to normal'** and what is very wrong about it: **no one cares.**
Sebastian Schulze

---

[2] Miyazaki, Hirokazu: Arbitraging Japan: dreams of capitalism at the end of finance, University of California Press, Berkley, 2013, ISBN 978-0-520-27347-4, p 1

Content Overview

Table of Content

1 Preface

1.1 Audience

This book is targeted **towards people that want to take control of their own banking** and gain (large and in the future complete) independence from the old financial institutions that charge more than necessary in transfer fees, commissions, and standing fees and once in a while still require to be bailed out at the taxpayers' expense.

This book explains the game changing properties of the **decentralized block chain technology** on the example of three block chain payment protocols. Reference will be made toward **how things work or don't work in the traditional system,** hopefully answering the question: Why you should get started and join what is not a "hype" but a genuine revolution that is affecting the businesses of banking, money transfer, foreign exchange, accounting and many more.

You might have already heard about Bitcoin (or Ripple) and want to gain a **deeper understanding of the properties** of those protocols or explore new features and possibilities. Then this book is for you.

You are hearing for the first time about this **new technology emerging** and are not sure whether to participate in "the hype" or not. Then this book is for you. Just beware it is not a "hype" it is a genuine socio-economic revolution unfolding.

You are one of those customers that are **fed up with their bank** and want to take the easy way out of a failing banking system tied to inflationary currencies. This book can serve as practical guide to help you make exactly that transition.

You are or have a company that is dealing with foreign business partners and or has subsidiaries abroad and "overseas" and **want to**

cut out exchange and bank fees for transferring your funds. This book has the answer.

Finally, there might be persons or institutions that want to use the Ripple and Stellar protocol to **trade and invest in digital currencies** (like Bitcoin) or the old national currencies (like the US Dollar or Yen and others) or metals like silver, gold and platinum.

This book will **describe** how to **set up accounts** and virtual wallets and how to use the Ripple and Stellar's in-built distributed exchange function to their full potential in buying and selling whatever valuables, assets or resources you can imagine.

No matter how much (or how little) you think you may know about Bitcoins and the other new payment protocols this book can show you **how to use and profit the most from this emerging technology and banking standard of the future**.

You are afraid of getting scammed or robbed? This book has a special chapter on **how to secure your wallets and accounts**, how to trade sound and safely with as much or little risk as you wish.

Be brave enough to be your own bank! Become financially independent and self-sufficient (by cutting out the middleman)!

1.2 Structure

In the **introduction** (Chapter 2) I will muddle (roughly) through the general properties of block chain based currencies and payment protocols. Also I will make reference to some properties of the **inner workings of Bitcoin and Ripple** when highlighting some of their advantages (open access, decentralized, digital, unforgeable).

I will keep the Chapter 3 **on the Bitcoin, Ripple and Stellar protocol** as short as possible. Firstly there are many good "Ultimate Guides", "101's", "**Introductions**" and indispensible "Manuals" etc. to Bitcoin out there already. "**Mastering Bitcoin**" by Mr.

Antonopoulos[3] sticks out as a technical description of the inner workings of the Bitcoin protocol geared towards those who understand at least some programming language.

Secondly Caveat Emptor Publishers already considers **publishing separate guides** on each currency and protocol (and major individual exchanges/gateways) in the **Financial Independence Basics Series** following Book 1 in the series (this book), to cover the whole ecosystem of modern digital currencies and service providers. (If you are interested in cooperating please contact >euauthor.gmail.com<.)

To my knowledge there is **no book out** yet dealing with Ripple or Stellar as trading and payment platforms. So explaining how **Ripple and Stellar** are different from Bitcoin and from each other is one aim of Chapter 3.

Chapter 4 "**How to protect yourself** from the greatest risks" offers an explanation of the major risks in using block chain based currencies and how to avert them.

Chapter 5 discusses in detail "Why **block chain based digital currencies are superior to traditional currencies** and how payments are processed" today in the legacy banking system.

Chapters 7 to 9 offer **additional resources**, including a **bibliography, link list and details of exchanges** and gateways.

You may directly go to any sub-chapter that you find interesting.

If you are looking to deepen or refresh your knowledge you will also find a **glossary** of important key words at the end of this book.

---

[3] Mr. Antonopoulos served as the head of the Anti Poverty Committee of the Bitcoin Foundation and as Chief Security Officer at the company Blockchain.info. His book "Mastering Bitcoin" is available at
 [http://www.amazon.com/Mastering-Bitcoin-Unlocking-Digital-Crypto-Currencies/dp/1449374042]

Interested to go beyond just reading? There is a short **video link list**, too.

1.3 Assumptions

You will not use this guide to **gamble away your life's savings** or that of your family. You understand that **I am not a financial expert** and that this book is for information purpose only. **At no time** I do give financial or **investment advice**. You comprehend that anything you choose to do or "not to do" - and in relation to the topic of this book and the information provided therein - you will do on **your own responsibility and risk**.[4]

For understanding the concepts explained and information provided in this book you will need to have a **minimum of prior knowledge** and some common sense concerning how the economy works. If you don't I recommend "Economix" by Goodwin et al (see literature list).

Also some **practical skill concerning the internet and normal banking** systems will be required. Ideally you have successfully used traditional online banking systems or bought something online with a credit card (for example this book). Having prior knowledge of PayPal or other internet payment systems the author of this book would consider you a tech-savvy power user already.

As this book will exemplify, doing the same with Bitcoin or the Ripple / Stellar protocols is much easier and less costly (time and money). Once wallets are set up, **sending and receiving money and trading becomes as easy as sending and receiving e-mail**.

---

[4] That what it means to be and independent human being. In the sense of "Sapere aude" it is however also every readers duty to step out of their self-incurred tutelage, to abandon their unfaithful stewards. If you are not willing to use your own brain this book is not for you.

2 Introduction

2.1 The most audacious currency since the Euro

"Today many people **have lost faith in the financial institutions** we've trusted for centuries. Some of our largest **banks have failed** and no longer exist. Those that survived needed **massive bailouts**. Citizens in some countries have lost their life savings to pay for **failed government decisions**. And for those who do find safety, the value of their savings is being drained by the **constant drip of inflation**. Our financial system is overdue for a reset."[5]

"There is **no denying** that the action (and inaction) of financial market professionals [...] have **resulted in catastrophic economic damage**. Yet **how should we respond** critically to this fact?"[6] asks Hirokazu Miyasaki in his book "Arbitraging Japan: Dreams of **Capitalism at the End of Finance**".

On the title page of this book you may find "Burn the banks" crossed out and in its stead replaced with "Join the currency revolution". That is to say: No, please do not go outside with a pitchfork and try burning down any bank. Damage to property or people is not in the intention of this book, no matter what banks, insurances, financial advisors, hedge fonds, raiders and weapons of financial mass destruction did to your country and loved ones.

Retribution is not the proper response nor is theorizing about what a proper critique would look like. There still is innovation in **financial technologies** but it is a kind of positively disrupting

---

[5] An anonymous statement on the website of the Distributed Autonomous Company BitSharesX
supporting its founding rational [https://bitshares-x.info/about.php] summarizing the rational for digital currencies and block chain based payment processing.
[6] Miyazaki, Hirokazu: Arbitraging Japan: dreams of capitalism at the end of finance, University of California Press, Berkley, 2013, ISBN 978-0-520-27347-4, p 6

innovation[7] that this book will discuss that is definitively not originating from the financial market professionals nor is it based in the academic sciences or a grand economic theory. **The coming financial revolution** is triggered and driven by "normal people" like you and me.

"Millionaire by Christmas" is crossed out, too. **Trying to get rich as long as the system permits** and on the cost of others and society as a whole isn't an acceptable thing. Unfortunately there are many "**Get rich quickly**" **systems and guides** out there trying to capitalize on the digital currency revolution. This book however **doesn't offer a subscription or fool proof system** to get rich. Instead this book tries to get you hooked on an **invested into an idea.**

Speculation, greed and instability are what the **current western legacy system** seems to stand for. Anyone into digital currencies for **short term gains** is in it for the wrong reason. The **promise** of digital currencies is not that much in their possible appreciation but their its property **to connect people and enable trade** in anything imaginable in ways that do **not rely on the authority** of and subordinance to the old system (l'acien regime).

2.2 Countries disappear - so do currencies

The author of this book was born in **a country that does not exist anymore** (the German Democratic Republic, the better Germany as it styled itself, but actually in many respects it wasn't). Its disappearance went largely unnoticed to the western financial world as its currency (the Eastern German Mark) was never much used outside of the country and naturally ceased to exist, when the country failed and joined the Federal Republic of Germany. My second currency (the German Mark) then again was abandoned in favor of **a third currency the Euro**.

---

[7] that is not somehow a continuation of the old ways of creating complex derivative products (that are potentially dangerous, because of their "dual use value")

Since the beginning of the First World War different regions in Germany **have seen more than eight different government issued currencies**[8] and multiple official legal tenders (and unofficial tenders) come and go. This included war money, emergency money, railway money, stamp and ration books, paper money being stamped "stable value" as well as private money experiments like the "Wära", etc.

Bresciani-Turroni remarks on the situation concerning **non-government issued currencies** during the times of German hyper-inflation[9]: "Illegal issues were especially frequent in the occupied territories. It is said that in the autumn of 1923 there were **two thousand different kinds of emergency money** in circulation".

As people lost trust in an ever inflating currency, the economy spiraled downwards. Some historians suggest that it was the economic troubles that virtually wiped out the middle class and triggered a process that led to the credibility crisis of the still fledgling German democracy.

With respect to government policy and inflation F. A. Hayek comments[10], "that **history is largely a history of inflation**, and usually of inflations **engineered by governments** and **for the gain of governments**".

Hyperinflation, currency reform and economic failure have repeatedly destroyed the life's-savings of millions of citizens, i.e. even

---

[8] Germany abandoned the gold standard as its currency basis in order to pay for the war effort in 1914. The USA abandoned its partial backing of the US Dollar by gold in 1972 to devalue the huge debts it amassed fighting an essentially agriculture based economy in South-East-Asia.

[9] C. Bresciani-Turroni, The Economics of Inflation, Augustus M. Kelley, New York, 1968 reprint of 1937 edition, pp. 341–345

[10] F. A. Hayek, Denationalization of Money: The Argument Refined, Institute of Economic Affairs, 1978, p34
[https://mises.org/sites/default/files/Denationalisation%20of%20Money%20The%20Argument%20Refined_5.pdf]

in the country that is now considered the economic power house of Europe. One lesson is that **stability and economic continuity cannot be taken as granted**. They are a rather pleasant exception to the otherwise turbulent economic and monetary history of countries and the world as a whole.

The latest **financial crisis and scandals** (subprime, Southern Europe, Cyprus, Libor fixing, to name just a few) are a reminder of the fact that even when there are no imminent disruptive pressures (i.e. civil war, resource depletion, natural disaster) our **financial sector is in itself instable** and if the persons who govern it could be trusted to always act in the public interest, their actions and policy does not always seem to produce results that are in the interest of the public.

The financial sector - and other industry sectors, too - are ruled by individuals that are led astray by **a system that creates the wrong incentives**. Accordingly we might be able to distinguish between good persons and bad systems but looking into the history of banking fraud and financial crimes and failed government policy the **instability and inability of control and oversight** of the world's financial and banking system **cannot be disputed**.

If we were to accept the simple fact that such control is indeed impossible or **too costly and restrictive if seriously attempted** we are now given to **opportunity to build a more open, transparent, safe and stable system**. A new financial and banking system that would allow our global economy and the people that drive it to **prosper and concentrate on innovation** rather than the administration of **systemic adversity**.

2.3 Enter Bitcoin

Mr Normand of JP Morgan calls Bitcoin: "**the most audacious**

currency since the Euro".[11] Bitcoin and other digital currencies present a viable **alternative to the way we transfer and store value**. An alternative our banks and credit card providers wished that could be regulated away or simply prohibited. It is a **technological and financial revolution** that is triggered by the rather simple invention of a digital distributed common ledger - the **block chain technology**.

While **record keeping at a central ledger** is not exactly a new thing but a very ancient practice[12] what makes the block chain technology revolutionary is combining this prudent accounting practice with the **networking infrastructure** that we use on an hourly basis - the internet.

Through the internet the common ledger becomes:

- publicly accessible (**anyone can participate** – no exclusion on financial or socio-political grounds).

- stored in its entirety on many computers and servers (**redundant**, decentralized, distributed, digital).

- unchangeable; its data entries **cannot be changed**, forged or deleted by any individual or authority (**truth, freedom, political independence**).

Critics point fingers to alternative currency scams, exchange failures, criminal exploits, theft and other issues which when examined properly in their scale and the **resulting damage to individuals** (and the stability of the financial system) are revealed to

---

[11] John Normand, JP Morgan, Global Rates & FX Research, 11 February 2014, "The audacity of bitcoin: Risks and opportunities for corporates and investors" (GPS-1319815-0)
[https://docs.google.com/file/d/0B0xHDZkxOzjMc0cwZFlqbGd4RzJNWkZldk p5QzBYUWFOTUhr/edit?pli=1]
[12] David Andolfatto, Vice President Federal Reserve Bank of St. Louis, 31.03.2014
[http://www.stlouisfed.org/dialogue-with-the-fed/assets/Bitcoin-3-31-14.pdf]

be microscopic compared to what is still going on in the traditional (government sanctioned) financial systems with for example cash, credit and derivatives.

Any **infrastructure can be misused,** but do we outlaw highways or motorcars because some people choose to drive without seat belts and much too fast?[13]

2.4 My experiment

By chance and very late actually, I heard about **Bitcoin,** the digital currency and its underpinning **block chain technology**. Andreas Antonopoulos[14] wrote a technical book about it ("Mastering Bitcoin") and Lynda.com (the online training and video learning brand) published a short introduction to Bitcoin ("Up and Running with Bitcoin"). Which I do recommend both as further reading and watching, together with the other books and sources in the literature list at the end of this book.

From the day the Bitcoin (and the block chain technology that carries it) was **conceived by Satoshi Nakamoto** (a pseudonym to hide the real identity of the creator) the number and possibilities for the application of digital currencies and their respective transfer protocols to real world problems have seen exponential growth and are at the **verge of widespread adoption** throughout different industries (not just in banking and finances).

I did the experiment myself and **bought my first Bitcoin(s)** to be stored in a desktop / offline wallet on my computer. I was intrigued

---

[13] Government have not even come around to prosecuting the financial professionals that have knowingly caused the subprime housing crisis in the United States of America that in turn had plunged the world economy into deep recession. Prosecutors do not have the stomach to go after professionals with money that know how to protect themselves. Our judicial systems have become a game of resource allocation. Justice is not served equally anymore.
[14] Mr. Antonopoulos, see above

by **how easy it was** and that I could do it all by myself without leaving the house or filling out endless paper forms. Then I read more about it and the **evolving landscape of the technology** behind that "virtual gold" as it is sometimes enthusiastically described by other authors and in the respective Bitcoin discussion forums.[15]

Through my small Bitcoin experiment I got into **contact with Ripple** (a second generation block chain based transfer protocol) that comes with its own unit of accounting the 'XRP' and later also with Stellar (another protocol and unit of accounting 'STR').

About 520 digital currencies are currently traded on major and minor (online) exchanges around the world. About 30 of those currencies do currently have a market capitalization of over USD 1 Million and thereby passed a strong proof of concept milestone. Most of those currencies are further developments of the block chain idea in their second and third generation or represent the **implementation of completely new ideas**. Bitcoin is currently noting a market capitalization of over USD 4800 Million. Ripple is valued at USD 141 Million.[16]

Though I am based in Europe, I have bought the equivalent of around USD 100 at a Ripple exchange in New Zealand, at about 30% under the current exchange rate and then transferred the currency to my Ripple online wallet.

What is so significant about this little experiment is that I have transferred my money **to the other side of the world and back**. I did take advantage of the difference in the exchange rate between my unit of accounting (the XRP) and a foreign currency - the USD. I did so without even knowing the meaning of the word 'arbitrage' (which

---

[15] Please find a list of dicussion forums and news providers in the link list / respective chapters at the end of this book.
[16] Data acquired from [http://coinmarketcap.com/currencies/views/all/] at 28.10.2014

is the technical term used by experienced traders for such a kind of transaction) - I only found out later.

The Ripple **transfer happened** almost instantly. Ripple's "block time" is **5 seconds** and transfer requests are often confirmed even faster than that. In comparison the withdrawal of the USD funds from the local (European) Ripple Gateway that I used to withdraw to my "real" bank account took about 2 days (using the European SEPA bank transfer system).

The **cost incurred** in buying and transferring the foreign currency to my wallet using the Ripple payment protocol was **insignificantly small**. The local gateway charges a 0.5% commission on Bitcoin trading, but this was not a trade in Bitcoins, but in XRP and USD instead. I could have **avoided almost all fees** completely if I did not withdraw to my local bank account later. The SEPA bank transfer itself did not incur any costs (to me).

I could have done the same buying Japanese Yen (JPY), Chinese Reminbi (CNY), Brazilian Real (BRL), **any other currency or even gold, silver or platinum** that is offered at the Ripple gateways and exchanges in different parts of the world - given an equally beneficial difference in the market rate.

Instead of trading for arbitrage between my own wallets and accounts at different markets I could also have transferred my money to another person's wallet in any country in order **to buy goods and services** or to invest in a **business opportunity**. I also could have avoided the intermediary exchanges, if I did **trade directly with another person**.

Am I a **banker** with a longstanding relationship to currency exchanges around the globe? Am I a **financial expert** working in a foreign investment company? No I am not. I am **just the regular guy from next door** with no special education whatsoever in the banking or investment trade. And now I am even writing a book about it because it is the right thing to do. If I can do it so anyone can.

2.5 The selling point of block chain based currencies

The selling point of block chain based currencies and Bitcoin in particular can be summarized as the following[17].

Unlike gold, Bitcoins are:

- Easy to transfer (at the ease of e-mail)

- Easy to secure (encrypted wallets and clients)

- Easy to verify (unforgeable = 0 counterfeit Bitcoins in circulation)

- Easy to granulate (up to 10^{-8})

Unlike other fiat currencies, Bitcoins are:

- Limited in supply (21 Million)

- Not controlled by a central institution (no single point of failure)

- Not debt-based liabilities (value token in itself)

Unlike electronic fiat currency systems, Bitcoins are:

- Potentially anonymous (pseudonymus to begin with)

- Cannot be frozen by the protocol (no political control)

- Faster to transfer (Bitcoin: 10 minutes block time, Ripple: 5 seconds)

- Cheaper to transfer (incomparable with the traditional system)

Imagine, if I had **asked my local branch** (of an international bank)

---

[17] [https://en.bitcoin.it/wiki/Myths]

to allow me to do the same (arbitrage trading or sending money to a foreign account to purchase goods).[18] Even if I could have convinced my bank to **allow me to do so** (or used a traditional online foreign exchange trading platform) I would have run into one or several of the following problems:

- set up a special foreign currency or trading account
- no provision of accurate market data by my bank
- fixed internal exchanges rate
- additional fees for exchange to a foreign currency
- no cooperating agreement or relationship with another bank in the market where I like buy and transact
- two or even three sets of intermediary banks (or enablers)
- prohibitively high transfer costs and fees
- "bucketing" of trades (especially at foreign exchange portals)[19]

The **opportunity would have vanished** before I even finished convincing my bank to go through all that trouble.

2.6 But I am perfectly happy the way things are

Using international **credit cards** instead has enabled many customers to actually **make international purchases** online[20] as long the seller accepts the particular card you were issued through your bank. What

---

[18] Very likely the personal at my local branch would have to look up the word 'arbitrage' in a dictionary first.

[19] Most forex houses "bucket" customer orders—accept them without executing any real trade. They charge spreads, commissions, interest, etc. for non-existent trades.

[20] The transfer of funds however only works (is limited to) between customer and merchants. A normal user cannot normally choose to become a receiver of funds. Peer-to-peer, customer to customer transfers are not possible. This essentially limits users of those system in their freedom of exchange with others.

most customers are not entirely aware of is that the credit cards **incur standing fees additionally to usage fees** rendered due when the card is used for domestic and foreign payments.

Customers are **double charged** (transfer fees and standing fees), but that is not where it ends. Whoever wants to accept payments with credit cards has to **pay a percentage** on the payments he receives (**swiping fees**) and sometimes additional standing fees for using a particular payment system and / or **renting payment processing hardware**, too.

In certain markets (e.g. Canada) **totally up to 4%** or more of the transaction volume is **"lost" in the payment processing chain** (charged as fees to senders and receivers). As major card issuers and payment processors charge "a sliding scale, so cost per unit falls as transaction volume increases"[21] receiving small or micro-payments actually makes no sense for many merchants. The dilemma merchants face is that the **trouble and fees outweigh the benefit** and payment received, yet customers demand to pay cashless and online not matter how small the amount.

Because merchants are charged by their payment processor and credit card company they have in turn **introduced surcharge (i.e. fees for card usage)**[22].

The **credit card companies that form an oligopoly** (e.g. in some countries Master Card and Visa card **dominate more than 90%** of the credit cards market) play the interest of each of their "customers" against one another. While banks and payment processors are able to (partially) **hand through some of those charges** and provide (unnecessary) additional services like insurances, **merchants** see their profit margins diminished and **resort to card surcharges**.

---

[21] Visa card website [http://www.visaeurope.com/about-us/fees-and-interchange]
[22] For example Easyjet (a European budget airline) is charging about EUR 8 per normal Visa card credit payment.

Sebastian Schulze

The payment processing industry in the United States of America is valued at about USD 460 Billion[23] Visa Card alone transfers about USD 3 Trillion per year.[24] One has to admit: the credit card brands' business model is **nothing short of ingenious**, though critics might call it predatory how the market was cornered and how merchants and customers are both **charged for exactly the same payment transfer**.

Sponsoring a bill to reduce the "highest international **swiping fees**" imposed by Visa and MasterCard in a single market, Senator Ringuette of the Banking Committee of the **Canadian Parliament** made the following **comment on the situation**[25]: "This committee […] received evidence from Bitcoin users that, first of all, the entire **virtual currency phenomenon was triggered** by people who were absolutely **tired of bank user fees and credit card fees**. […] From my perspective, I see that, whether it's Bitcoin or, eventually, another virtual currency, **it's an innovative product**, just like 40 years ago when Visa and MasterCard started the fantastic plastic. It was an innovative product. So **you'll have to face competition**. From my perspective, I'm kind of happy about that."

Thanks to the **block chain technology, new payment protocols** like Ripple and Stellar domestic and international transfers **no matter how small or big in volume may take only seconds**.

Those facts alone (**speed, nearly zero fees, ignorance towards the**

---

[23] Brian Kelly, The Bitcoin Big Bang: How Alternative Currencies Are About to Change the World, 2014, p71
[24] [http://bankinnovation.net/2014/10/ripple-ecosystem-expands-with-british-startup-ripula/]
[25] Transcript of the Proceedings of the Standing Senate Committee on Banking, Trade and Commerce, Parliament of Canada, Issue 15 - Evidence - October 8, 2014,
[http://www.parl.gc.ca/Content/SEN/Committee/412/banc/15ev-51627-e.htm?Language=E&Parl=41&Ses=2&comm_id=3] video available:
[http://www.youtube.com/watch?v=xUNGFZDO8mM]

volume to be transferred, ignorance of jurisdiction, availability to everyone with internet access) appear nothing less than **life-threatening to an industry** that has successfully **evaded innovation and customer service** for much too long.

Though such industry can always choose to **adapt to a new technology or try fighting it**. Who could have imagined such a historic reversal of roles, the normal customer demanding new technology and innovation to be introduced while current **financial elites** may possibly take the position of **Luddites**.[26]

2.7 The digital currency revolution

The way **peer to peer communication** and data exchange has revolutionized the internet; **digital currencies are about to revolutionize the financial and banking system**. Bitcoin is sometimes called to be to the financial industry what MP3 sharing was to the music industry. The difference is that Bitcoin is an internationally decentralized protocol that runs on the internet infrastructure and not a company (like for example Napster) that can be sued into bankruptcy.

One might argue we are witnessing nothing smaller than the **establishment of the world's first universally and globally accepted digital currency** and payment system based on the simple idea of common digital and distributed ledger. The future will show.

Using new platforms like Bitcoin or Ripple and their respective wallets and exchanges it is already **possible to transfer funds** (internationally) and have them arrive **within seconds at costs near zero**. But the technology has even more to offer in terms of possible applications. Whereas Bitcoin was initially seen as an alternative currency and "virtual gold", we now see the new payment protocols

---

[26] Because among others this technological innovation is vastly disruptive to most banking business models.

and alternative virtual currencies as platforms for the **introduction of a vast array of innovative applications**.

The users of the new digital currencies; block chain based currencies in particular share a vision of a new financial world. A world where **value is transferred and protected** without the need to trust a failing centralized system (or any other party). Precisely, a world that **will never need bailouts**. A world that offers an equal playing field where all transactions are transparent but the user's financial life can stay private. A world **without arbitrary interference or exclusion**: a world where everyone can participate and share the benefits equally. A world **not limited by borders, business hours, or location**. "What would be possible if we could create this kind of world?"[27]

The choice is yours to **further support a failing system** with your fees, that is in our case centralized banking and the extortious credit card system **or be your own bank** and store **and exchange money freely** at nearly no cost between peers and equals. No matter what, the world's financial and currency system will surely look different in 2020 (6 years from now).

2.8 Be brave enough to be your own bank

"Bitcoin is not the new money for internet, but it is the **new internet for money, value and ownership in all forms**. Crypto currencies like Bitcoin are the next step in the **emancipation of all world citizens**, and can help create a new dynamic for democracy, society and economy." Lykle de Vries[28]

Currency, payment protocol, future innovative applications and world financial and monetary implications aside what is most

[27] Paragraph adapted from BitSharesX [https://bitshares-x.info/about.php] summarizing the rational for digital currencies and block chain based payment processing.
[28] [http://cointelegraph.com/news/112842/bitcoin-101-understanding-the-real-value-of-the-blockchain]

fascinating about the idea of a distributed common ledger is that **it enables and carries democracy, participation, free speech and freedom of association** over borders to people who are currently denied such freedoms through barriers and high costs of participation.

"Be brave enough to use your own mind", Immanuel Kant once wrote. Given that Bicoin and other block chain based currencies are long beyond a proof of concept we need to declare: **Be brave enough to be your own bank** and exchange freely with others around you. Be brave enough to use this book as a starting point of your own journey towards a more **self-determined life.**

In the 1780s Kant tried answering the question **"What is enlightenment"** at a time when it was essentially going on for about 100 years already.[29] In our case **this book is a little faster**. Bitcoin has been around since 2009 and Ripple since 2012.

Many users and customers still need to **ask themselves the question what is money** and do we really need to limit ourselves to what banks and governments claim it to be? Can we not be trusted to see and think ourselves? Why engage **any third party** which only **"contribution" is to charge additional fees**.

Until now there has been no way around banks, credit card companies and other payment processors with storing and exchanging money and making (regular) payments internationally or in international remittance and investment. **We can be trusted to exchange cash**, buying groceries in the next supermarket. Why shouldn't we be allowed to **exchange freely and directly in international markets** buying currency, assets, shares, resources, gold, invest in companies and business ideas alike, etc.

---

[29] Immanuel Kant, Beantwortung der Frage: Was ist Aufklärung?, Berlinische Monatsschrift, 1784

Peer to peer technology has broken new ground and forced the established industry to adopt new business models. Commercially successful **media platforms** that provide streaming or download of music and movies (like Hulu, Netflix, i-tunes, Amazon direct video and many others) are the **direct result** and example of their illegal predecessors making the business case, among other providing higher cost-efficiency and customer retention.

For a long time it seemed unimaginable that peer to peer and streaming technology could **enter mainstream business**, legislation was introduced, single companies and individuals were criminalized, but as a whole **"peer to peer" proved more resilient** and its economic **efficiency has prevailed**.

As command and control and its enforcement has proven inefficient big studios and **content owners move closer to the market** "where the consumer is" by **properly licensing content** to be provided online and at rates that the market responds to. The lesson that **you cannot fight your customers' wishes** and preferences was hard learned in that industry in particular.

Similarly to the previous achievements of peer to peer technology, we might also see what is going on with the new digital currencies as **a coming of age**, the emancipation of consciousness from an immature state of ignorance and **undeserved trust** towards a traditional, centralized, authoritarian system - a system that encouraged its insiders and elites to do the wrong thing.

The legacy system encouraged the **abuse of (insider) knowledge and power for private gain,** facing viable alternatives it has chosen to continue inefficient, time consuming and **overly costly procedures**. Because of those incentives whole countries and their populations suffered the consequences yet the financial institutions whose culture caused it, were bailed out at the cost of the normal tax payer.

It is a painful truth that for example in the United Stated the normal taxpayer bailed out the very institutions that caused so many citizens to lose their home.

Profit is privatized and when risk turns into liabilities it is socialized. Whole countries saw their credit rating drop overnight (several levels) and the burden of impeding bankruptcy was unloaded on population strata that could not logically, morally and legally be claimed to have had any fault in it.

Merchants and financial institutions are just starting to explore and to understand the **game changing character of Bitcoin**, the block chain technology and especially the Ripple payment protocol that allows the user **to trade in anything at nearly zero cost**.

The repercussions for the traditional banks and their business model are tremendous. New storage and payment providers, gateways, exchanges, enablers based on those new payment protocols are **attracting venture capital from all over the world** and promise to provide access, financial stability and self-determination to those that are not deemed worthy of financial services by the current system and that couldn't even effort the rates of a normal bank account or are excluded from the reach of its infrastructure.

Imagine **online payment without the need for credit cards** happening at nearly zero fees. Envision micro and macro payments across borders, international transfers from and to remote countries and regions at the lowest fees regardless of your social status or citizenship (including foreign currency exchange at global market rates). All of that is happening right now with the new systems and it is happening without most of the established banks.

Kant's essay ("Beantwortung der Frage: Was ist Aufklärung?) was a shrewd, **political challenge to men and women**, suggesting that the mass of **"domestic cattle"** have been bred, by **unfaithful stewards**, to **not question what they have been told about the**

world and its ways.[30]

The only proper way, to do it better this time is to **bring democracy into our elitarian and authoritarian financial systems**. This however can only happen if the user and customer stops to allow himself to be treated as cattle and starts **questioning how things are done**. Enlightenment in financial terms and (block chain based) procedures do have the power to bring democracy into current financial institutions. "Never again" shall the power to screw up so gigantically be concentrated in the hands of so few.

The following chapters of this book introduce essential properties of three digital currencies and payment protocols (Bitcoin, Ripple and Stellar), how they work in particular, how they are different from each other and the traditional system.

---

[30] http://en.wikipedia.org/wiki/Sapere_aude

3 Examples of block chain based currencies

3.1 Bitcoin

How it works

Mr Normand of JP Morgan calls Bitcoin: "**the most audacious currency since the Euro**".[31] While the Euro is somehow a supra-national currency unit that replaced 18 individual national currencies with the European Monetary Union, Bitcoin it is a stateless, digital, decentralized and peer to peer currency and payment protocol not issued or maintained by any national entity.

The 'hype' about Bitcoin is incredible, some proponents go as far as suggesting while the Euro replaced 18 national currencies, Bitcoin too has the **potential to replace some of the worlds currencies** (either completely or at least partially in international trade for example). In fact there are countries like Ecuador and the Philippines that openly contemplate introducing (national) digital currencies based on the block chain technology.

Bitcoin is called a **crypto-currency** because it uses a cipher (an algorithm used for encryption) to encrypt and thereby secure transactions and to control the creation of new Bitcoins. The backbone of Bitcoin is its source code. Its source code determines which algorithm is used for encryption, how (currency) units are transferred and how individual network nodes and **users communicate through the payment protocol**.

The Bitcoin code and software is maintained by a network of

---

[31] John Normand, JP Morgan, Global Rates & FX Research, 11 February 2014, "The audacity of bitcoin: Risks and opportunities for corporates and investors" (GPS-1319815-0)
[https://docs.google.com/file/d/0B0xHDZkxOzjMc0cwZFlqbGd4RzJNWkZldk p5QzBYUWFOTUhr/edit?pli=1]

programmers rather than a central bank or single country or company. Bitcoin's source code is publicly available (**it is open source**) and "the code quality and clarity is head and shoulders above most commercial code-bases".[32]

Anyone can install and run the software, become part of the **Bitcoin network,** "mine" and thereby "supply" Bitcoins. Calculation difficulty and therefore necessary computing power (hardware and electricity) that is required to be a successful miner rise over time, in the long term. This process is deliberately designed to **resemble the activity of mining gold** and accessing ever deeper and more difficult to mine deposits. Henceforth the notion of calling Bitcoin "**digital gold**".

There is however a more fundamental purpose to this **"mining" process** than just simulating the decreasing but steady supply of four gold mines to the digital currency world. By solving complex mathematical equations the miners (i.e. the network nodes) compete **to verify the transactions** that are entered over the network.

The **energy and computing power** used to solve difficult calculations (algorithms) depends on how much the Bitcoins are currently worth. While mining difficulty increases in the long run it is flexible in the short term to **balance the cost** (for users) **and profitability** (for miners) of the protocols' payment processing.[33]

The **verification of a transaction** takes place at many nodes simultaneously and results in an agreement (consensus) of the majority of the modes. The thus verified transaction gets entered in a block of verified transactions (blocks are written continuously every

---

[32] http://www.reddit.com/r/Bitcoin/comments/1zb8ip/analyzing_the_bitcoinqt_source_code/cfscd4q
[33] Brian Kelly concludes, "The computing power and energy needed to solve the math problem serves as a cost to sending a false message." Brian Kelly, The Bitcoin Big Bang: How Alternative Currencies Are About to Change the World, 2014, p 53

10 minutes).

>>Bitcoins never leave the block chain<<

All blocks together form the chain of blocks and constitute the **common ledger** that tracks every transaction from the very first one. The block chain is the actual place where individual Bitcoins and fractions of it are linked to a **public address**[34] (a user that owns them). Bitcoins never actually leave the ledger and therefore are very traceable. The transaction of Bitcoins to another address (another user) requires confirmation with the **private key** of the current owner. Funds are then reassigned to the other address (other user) on the ledger through the verification process.[35]

The main purpose of mining therefore is to constitute a **decentralized computing network to verify transactions.** For the **verification of a block** of transactions the miner (individual network node) is rewarded with Bitcoins according to a declining yield schedule (as if mining gold) and is given a negligible and voluntary transaction/verification fee (to create a further **incentive to process verifications** even at times when the normal **mining reward** has declined to strongly or for the **prioritization of individual transactions**).

As everyone can start mining and **verifying a block of transactions** but the reward of Bitcoins is only awarded to the one that finishes it first, **mining pools** have formed to bundle computing power and to even out the returns of their activity. The major appeal of this process of **competitive decentralized verification of transactions** is that it significantly reduces **transaction costs** for payments and establishes the payments system **security against fraud** (and for

---

[34] A Bitcoin address is a string of letters and numbers 24 to 26 digits long [https://en.bitcoin.it/wiki/Address]
[35]
[http://cointelegraph.com/news/111680/btc_101_the_beginner_s_guide_to_unde rstanding_bitcoin]

example hacking). Even if an individual network node becomes compromised (hacked) and would send out falsified data, the network would simply overrule its "minority opinion".

This automatic nature and **safety of the transaction verification** is important to highlight as there is the misunderstanding around that a community of Bitcoin volunteers and users would conduct an (ad hoc) majority vote on each transaction. Yes, network nodes and miners are volunteers in the sense that they do not work for a payment processing company but they are also **paid automatic verification processors**. Transaction verification takes place automatically and follows a **secure and predetermined procedure** after the Bitcoin protocol.

The verification process ensures that the entire network agrees on which public address holds how many Bitcoins at any given time, proof of it is the historic record in the (transaction) block chain. **No single hacker could create or forge Bitcoins** as they do only exist on that common ledger.

Each miner has **a copy of the whole chain** of transaction blocks that where ever created - **the whole block chain** - on his computer. So it is for their service of verifying transaction and also **record keeping** that miners are receiving "new" Bitocins and fees.[36]

Any individual or business with internet access can be a Bitcoin user and **execute transfers directly** with any other user. Bitcoin **excludes no one**. Bitcoin does **not restrict access**. Bitcoin does **not require** any prior **authorization** to transact nor does it require verification of the users identity. The network only verifies the transaction data (i.e. public key(s), the private key of the sender and the amount).

-

---

[36] The details of transaction fees and mining rewards are thoroughly explained at [http://bitcoinfees.com/]

Using bitcoin wallets the user is assigned an electronic address (**the public address**) that is the user's "Bitcoin account number" and a password to this account (**the private key**) to enable you to send out Bitcoins. This is essentially all that is needed to interact with the Bitcoin protocol, receive and transfer funds.

To receive and transfer every user must however **open a wallet** (either online or download a wallet software that is available for different devices and operating systems) that is **for free**.

Bitcoin itself does not require the user to give up any additional identifying information (name, phone number, physical or IP address). Most online wallet providers therefore speak about **anonymity** with regard to Bitcoin while in fact it is "only" a **pseudonymous system** (every user is assigned a static public address that can be looked up in the public common ledger). While an individual address is static, **any user may create as many addresses as he wants**.

Since **"everyone" has a copy of the blockchain** (or can explore it online or follow it in real time), anyone can go over the history of all transactions and see what public address sent how much and where to. Bitcoin **transactions are easily traceable** anyone can track Bitcoins as they move from one public address to the next.

The user's **identity is not revealed** as long he himself does not give up additional identifying information to third parties that could be used to match transactions. **Anonymity of the user's identity is easily lost** once the user's public key is connected to exchanges where he did trade and link a traditional bank account for withdrawal or leave other indentifying data.

Opening a Bitcoin wallet - Clients

If you have some programming skills you can directly communicate with the Bitcoin protocol using the **raw transaction API** or even write yourself a little program that is automating your payment needs with Bitcoin, using the proper commands and accessing all the functions of the system. This is one advantage of open source protocols, if the user knows how to communicate directly **the user is allowed to do so.**[37]

Luckily for the **common user** opening a wallet does not require any special or programming skills apart from **navigating the internet and using standard desktop clients safely**. The programming community surrounding Bitcoin has come up with many different and **safe client solutions**. Users have the choice to download a **user client** and run it from their computer or mobile phone, or to access an online wallet. Currently those are the main ways of participating in Bitcoin, but many more possibilities do exist and are evolving.[38]

The best way to start using Bitcoin clients is in first visiting the **"Choose your own wallet website"** [https://bitcoin.org/en/choose-your-wallet]. This is the website of the **Bitcoin Foundation**, that is the community of programmers (and normal users) that maintain the system.

The website offers you a choice of many different **wallet applications** that are maintained and programmed by other communities or companies, some of them open source and decentralized like Bitcoin, some of them proprietary and using a central server structure to direct transfers to the Bitcoin network.

If you want to stay true to the **"Bitcoin philosophy"** you would choose an **open source, direct access and securely encrypted solution**. You can choose to install a client on your mobile phone (Android, iOS, Blackberry) or your computer (Windows, Mac, Linux). Also a choice of web clients - that can be accessed through any internet browser - is listed.

---

[37] [https://en.bitcoin.it/wiki/Raw_Transaction]
[38] [http://www.coindesk.com/information/how-to-store-your-bitcoins/]

I do not recommend any application or client in particular. The Bitcoin Wiki keeps a regularly updated **list comparing the properties** of the available solutions [https://en.bitcoin.it/wiki/Clients].

However **making your first quick steps** into Bitcoin would I suggest you start with 'MultiBit' which is a desktop wallet program that **is light weight** and does not require you download the whole block chain. It is available for Windows, Mac and Linux. After the install from [https://bitcoin.org/en/choose-your-wallet] you can intuitively **create your first wallet**. Once you have created a wallet with 'MultiBit' you can now see and copy your **public address** as a string of letters and also as QR code.

Bitcoin addresses are a string of 26 to 34 alphanumeric characters, starting with the numbers 1, 2 or 3. A **Quick Response Code** (QR) is a black and white dot matrix picture that is more easily scanned by phones and other computers and offers additional checksum and redundancy for a more error safe exchange of addresses between users).

Example of a Bitcoin address[39]:
3J9Qt1lpEZ13CNmQviecSnyiWrnqRhWNLy

Example of a Bitcoin address with destination tag (as used by some exchanges internally):
3J9Qt1lpEZ13CNmQviecSnyiWrnqRhWNLy?dt=12345

Exchanges and web applications that trade in Bitcoin or offer online wallets may assign funds to an **individual address**. Some exchanges however choose to put all funds in a **common wallet**. Individual user's funds are then distinguished and accounted for by an additional destination tag that is added after the common wallet's

[39] This is a hypothetical example, do not use it to send any funds to it, those funds would be lost, most likely however the address will be rejected by the protocol through a checksum test

public address (e.g. "?dt=12356").

The user's public address (with or without destination tag) is everything that is needed to buy and receive Bitcoins. Bitcoins are most safely put into the user's individual wallet (without destination tag).

Bitcoin Exchanges

Currently a Bitcoin is exchanged for around USD 320 at different **Bitcoin exchanges**.[40] Those exchanges and gateways serve to connect the traditional banking and currency system as they do **change traditional currency into digital currencies** and vice versa. Most exchanges support a variety of digital currencies and traditional fiat currency pairs to be traded or directly exchanged.

Opening an account at (for example) the Bitstamp or SnapSwap exchanges[41] any user can **transfer initial funds** from a traditional bank account into the account at the exchange via **normal bank transfer** (ACH/SEPA).

Most exchanges however require users to go through **additional 'Know your customer' (KYC) or 'Anti-Money-Laundering' (AML) procedures** prior to depositing traditional currency. Such procedures force the user to submit **proofs of identity and residence** (a copy of an ID or passport and a utility letter with the current living address) during registration or before funds can be deposited.

Once Bitcoins have been bought at the exchange the users can (and should) **withdraw** them to their **personal wallet** (e.g. Multibit). The user is also advised that for the purpose of long-term storage of

---

[40] Look for up to date rates at for example [http://bitcoincharts.com/] or [http://coinmarketcap.com] or [https://winkdex.com/]

[41] I do not recommend a particular exchange. A list of several exchanges and gateways is given at the end.

substantial funds a new public address should be created and **taken completely offline** (e.g. USB wallet, paper wallet, memory wallet, hardware wallet)[42].

Leaving Bitcoins **in the account of an exchange** they actually represent an **IOU of the exchange** (like traditional giro money). Only by withdrawing Bitcoins into the user's wallet they enter the block chain under the user's **own public address** (as opposed to the address of the exchange with destination tag) and thereby become a truly **independent value token**.

If on the next day all banks and exchanges went bankrupt the Bitcoins would still be there on the block chain and **nobody else could access them** besides the user and rightful owner with his **private key**. And even then **without banks** and exchanges (and even without governments) users could **still directly exchange** their Bitcoins for goods and services with each other and an **efficient market rate** for Bitcoins would form from those transactions **allowing economic exchange to continue**.

That is even **in the absence of bank, exchanges and even governments** (providing laws), the business economy and **private exchange could still be functioning**. The only fragility and dependency of this payment system is that it **requires a working internet connection** and respective infrastructure. It is assumed that there are computers or mobile clients and the internet (or an ad hoc network) that connects them. Finally to verify transactions a sufficient number of **Bitcoin network nodes** (miners) must be accessible (being online, running the software).

---

[42] Some types of wallets are listed at [https://en.bitcoin.it/wiki/Wallet] a lengthy description on how to secure them is also given at [https://en.bitcoin.it/wiki/Securing_your_wallet]

3.2 Ripple

How it works

While Ripple makes use of a central ledger, Ripple's philosophy with regard to mining and **value independence** sets it apart from Bitcoin. Ripple and Bitcoin both being block chain based crypto-currencies are in the end **very different things**.

Ripples are **pre-mined** and transactions are verified by a **special consensus algorithm** instead of mining work. Ripple's focus is on being a **platform to facilitate trade** in any currency or asset (traditional, fiat, digital, including Bitcoin, metals, resources, etc.) and is built on the insight that our current financial system by large moves around **units of accounting**.

Those units (most of the time) represent **the debt and liability of someone else**. That is most of the time we are moving around IOUs ('I owe you' promises). Some persons and institutions can be trusted to fulfill their promise and repay the debt but on a general basis **not all liabilities (of the same type) are the same**. Ripple (unlike Bitcoin) does not attempt to change the basis of or current financial and monetary system but provides the most fast, cost-efficient and less risky way to (continue to) run it.

"Perhaps the most important thing we need to realize about **bank deposits** is that they **are liabilities**. When you pay money into a bank, you don't really have a deposit... you have lent that money to the bank. They owe it to you. It becomes one of their liabilities. That's why we say our **accounts are in credit**: we have extended credit to the bank. Similarly, if you are overdrawn and owe money to the bank, that becomes **your liability and their asset**." Richard

Brown, IBM UK[43]

The traditional financial system basically only transfers obligations and promises for repayment around from central bank accounts through commercial accounts to cooperate and private accounts.

Like Bitcoins rest in the Bitcoin block chain, Ripples can be withdrawn to the **native Ripple client** but in respect to the movement of liabilities Ripple is no different from the traditional system. However Ripple encourages the user to first **consider whose obligations are dealt with** and who it is that is to be trusted.

Ripple essentially moves IOUs that are measured against its internal unit of accounting, the XRP. Instead of being led to believe (i.e. by the traditional banking institutions) that when buying and selling foreign currency and storing it in a foreign currency depot or an account with our bank, we do own real foreign currency, **Ripple is straight** and forthcoming right from the beginning that **we actually will only own an IOU** by a certain exchange and issuer to pay out that currency when we choose so.

Ripple is very explicit in that point, that before starting to trade the **user needs to assign a line of trust** with the respective trading partner (the exchange) that will become an issuer to the user for each type of IOU that the user chooses to trust and buy. Ripple gives each user **full control over the relationship** with each exchange by allowing the **trust line to be limited** in its amount for each type (of IOU) that is issued by an exchange.

In the Ripple payment system the internal unit of accounting, the **XRP** is assigned the function of a neutral basis currency that is trusted and **accepted by all market participants**. But users do **not need to buy the XRP in order to directly move funds**. Compared

---

[43] Richard Gendal Brown, Ripple is hard to understand, but it's worth making the effort: there's a deep insight at its core, at his blog "Thoughts on the future of finance" [http://gendal.wordpress.com/category/ripple/]

to Bitcoin this direct trade functionality (of whatever you trust) allows the user to avoid eventual price fluctuation of the internal unit of accounting (XRP).

A special feature of the Ripple protocol is to facilitate Rippling of IOUs of the same type, i.e. the moving of funds between different but equally or sufficiently trusted issuers may occur to improve the liquidity of a particular issuer/ market. This ability to automatically move IOUs of the same type to where they are in demand **increases market liquidity**.

As it may sound scary that the protocol may chose to start moving around the user's funds between issuers for that process to occur the user **needs to give explicit consent.** The individual user retains full control over Rippling to to occur when setting up the trust line and amount for each type of IOU and issuer (i.e. initially the check box 'allow rippling' is unchecked).

Ripple gateways register **offers** that users have made **to buy or sell** currencies (currency IOUs). Those offers are public commitments to trade one type of IOU for another at a fixed rate. Those commitments are written into the **order book** of the gateway. The order book becomes a **global marketplace for ask and bid offers** that is open to everyone.

The **Ripple Trade client** allows the user to send any currency IOU to anyone else even in the form of a different currency IOU, given that the receiving user trusts a particular issuer and currency pair. Ripple exchanges that also offer **gateway functionality can be integrated / added to the web client**. For the purpose of trading with gateways the user does not need to open separate accounts with exchanges, unless he prefers a certain exchange that is not offering integrated gateway function.

The user can choose for example to send CNY (Chinese Reminbi) even if the user only holds a balance of Euro funds in the Ripple account. Submitting a send CNY order the Ripple protocol, it automatically **finds the best exchange rate** for the transaction, possibly exchanging your Euros into other third currencies or the native XRP before arriving at CNY. If the protocol finds no direct way of conversion a **chain of conversion** can be created through third currencies arriving at the desired target currency at the **best rate the market provides** momentarily.

Users therefore can use the Ripple protocol to **execute and order payments in currencies they do not hold** to other users that are located anywhere else or buy any specific currency IOU as investment. The exchange rate is always the best available rate at the gateway markets. The **transfer cost incurred is minimal** (only intended to prevent abuse via spamming / DDoS).

Opening a Ripple wallet and exchanging currencies and other assets

A Ripple wallet is usually opened by using the native online client ("**Ripple Trade**") at [https://www.rippletrade.com/#/login]. Ripple Trade also offers Two-factor authentication (2FA) via short message to your phone (for additional security).

Opening an account the user is assigned a **public Ripple address**. Like the Bitcoin address, Ripple addresses are a string of letters and numbers. While Bitcoin addresses are a string of 26 to 34 alphanumeric characters, starting with the numbers 1, 2 or 3, public addresses in Ripple are generally of 34 characters and start with the letter "r".[44]

Ripple has introduced **Ripple names** that are linking to public Ripple addresses. Those Ripple names start with a tilt "~" and can otherwise be chosen freely by each user (if not already assigned). Ripple names compress the complicated alphanumeric public

---

[44] [https://wiki.ripple.com/Accounts]

addresses into **easy to remember and more individual identifiers** while retaining the full functionality[45] of the public address they link to (in a similar way domain names are linked to IP addresses).

Example of a Ripple (public) address as assigned by the native Ripple client[46]:
rfe8yiXUymTPx35BEwGjhfkaLtgNsTywxT

Example of a Ripple address with destination tag (as used by some exchanges internally):
rWeSsiXUymThJk3BEwQjhfkaLtgNsTyPol?dt=12345

Examples of Ripple names, that would link to different Ripple address:
~JohnDoe, ~ACMEcorp, ~RenderUntoCeasar, ~ResearchFund

Exchanges that are part of the Ripple network may assign funds to an **individual Ripple address** that is created newly for each registered user (e.g. Kraken). Some exchanges however choose to put all funds in a **common wallet**. Individual user's funds are then distinguished and accounted for by an additional destination tag that is added after the common wallet's public address (e.g. "?dt=12356").

Once added, different gateways can be selected within the Ripple Trade client's menu (Exchange -> Trade, Change market) to **sell or buy XRP** against another currency (IOU) in that market.

Trading means **creating offers to buy or sell** that are entered into the order book of the respective gateway that the user has chosen to trade in. Orders are executed when there is another offer in the **order book** (by another trader) that matches the user's entry.

---

[45] Full functionality that is except the checksum, so every user must be aware that transpositions or simple writing errors would send funds to a different account that might not be willing to send them back.

[46] The following addresses and Ripple names are hypothetical examples, do not use them to send any funds to, those funds would likely be lost. The example of the public address will likely be rejected by the protocol's checksum test.

Orders containing larger amounts may take some time to be fulfilled depending on whether there are enough matching offers issued by other traders that do match the user's offer in volume and price. Larger orders might also be only **partially executed** if the **market price moves** quicker than it takes to fulfill the respective order (i.e. when the order book runs out of matching offers, a sign for low liquidity of the market). Orders in the Ripple Trade client therefore are orders limited by the price the user assigned to it (**limit orders in general**).

Choosing to **convert** instead (Exchange -> Convert) will allow you to immediately convert any volume of currency or asset (IOU) the user has to any another currency or asset (IOU) of the user's choice finding the best (cheapest) rate and route among all added and sufficiently trusted gateways / currencies. Conversion orders are executed always entirely (whole volume) yet the "best rate" of the conversion result is forecasted with a $\pm$ **1% margin**, requiring the users consent to such possible deviation.

Sending (Send) requires the user to enter a public Ripple address or Ripple name you like to send funds to and allows the user to choose any gateway issued currency or asset (IOU) as the unit.

Unfortunately I might also happen that the user's conversion or send **request is denied,** that is the Ripple Trade Client will show you a message asking you to "Please make sure your account has enough funds, and a trust line to a [currency you want to convert to] gateway".

Given that the user **definitively has enough funds** and has assigned **more than sufficient trust** to all major gateways for that particular currency, that claim can mean that the **market has at that time not enough liquidity** to match the volume of the request or possibly that the gateways themselves have limited (or all together **suspended**) the amount they allow to be converted via a single request / for a certain type of IOU.

Ripple Gateways

Ripples (XRP) can be bought at **exchanges that trade Ripples**. Bitstamp (for example) is an exchanges that can be used to deposit funds from a traditional bank account and to buy Ripples directly.

Deposited funds have then become IOUs of the particular exchange (e.g. Bitstamp.USD) and can be transferred directly to the user's Ripple address or can be sold and exchanged to for XRPs. When considering **to buy XRPs directly** and within the online client of the exchange (e.g. Bitstamp) the user should be aware that this constitutes a **private sale between individual peers** (the exchange owner and the user) and happens outside the larger general market.

One must distinguish between the function of the exchange **to facilitate trade between many users** on the open market (Ripple node / gateway) and the direct to user (private) sale function of the exchange. Unaware of this distinction the user might unwittingly enter a direct sale of XRP at a rate that is above **the rate of the general market**. (Yes, it happened to this author!)

Funds should always be transferred to the user's public Ripple address (to their account at the **Ripple Trade client**). This transfer is virtually free. Ripple charges a negligible fee of XRP 0.00001 as an anti-spamming measure and to prevent denial-of-service (DDoS) attacks on the system.

Using the native Ripple Trade client the user can add the public address (or names and domain names) of the exchanges that also operate as a Ripple gateway and thereby access the order book of collected bids and asks at that gateway directly through the Ripple Trade client.[47] This then constitutes the **built-in distributed exchange**, and the user can avoid opening separate accounts with

---

[47] A list of exchanges and their addresses is provided at the end of this book. Also a list of gateways is available from Ripple [https://support.ripplelabs.com/hc/en-us/articles/202847686-Gateway-Information]

those exchanges, unless he prefers a certain exchange that is not a gateway or wants to use those exchanges to **withdraw funds** or deposit through the traditional banking system (ACH / SEPA).

The **Ripple Knowledge Center** offers a very detailed description on how to add gateways and assign trust [https://ripple.com/guide-to-currency-trading-on-the-ripple-network/].

The user needs to **assign a line of trust** with the gateway for each the type of currency (IOU). The gateway will then become an issuer to the user of the type of currency that the user chooses to trust and buy. This is done by adding the **public address of the exchange** (Log-in -> Funds -> Gateways -> Connect Gateway) for each currency pair to be traded.

The XRP, the native currency of the network and is automatically issued and trusted by all participants. For all other currency pairs the Ripple Trade client gives each user **full control over the relationship with each exchange** by allowing the trust line to be limited in its amount for each type of currency that is issued and for Rippling to occur or not.

3.3 Stellar

How it works

Stellar works very much like Ripple with a few exceptions. A co-founder of Ripple - that left Ripple - founded Stellar. The main difference for the user is that **Stellar's money supply increases** at the fixed a rate of **1% each year** and that **exchanges are trusted at once** for all the currencies they issue **when they are added**. Also Stellar is not run as a company for profit (like Ripple) but as a **non-profit organization** and has pledged to **give away most** of the pre-mined **Stellars** (STR) to users and (other) charitable organizations who **open and verify accounts**. Besides that Stellar is very similar to its predecessor Ripple and time will show which of the two will become more widely used.

The major difference between Stellar and its predecessor Ripple is mostly in monetary policy and charitable versus cooperate licensing and outlook. The inner workings and intended usability (to become the preferred transfer method of the financial system) is largely identical.

Opening a Stellar wallet

Users register an account with the **native Stellar online client** [https://launch.stellar.org/#/login]. Verifying themselves (optionally) with their **Facebook account users receive Stellars** (STR) for free. The earlier the user joined the more Stellars were distributed to the new account. Currently it is about **STR 200** that can be received upon verification that is a give-away value of about USD 0.4 at current exchange rates for every new user.

That means Stellar can be used right after registration (and after adding Stellar gateways) for trading. Depositing additional funds follows the same procedure as with Ripple, just that instead of Ripple gateways, **Stellar gateways are used** to deposit more funds through the legacy bank system. Certain exchanges offer both Ripple and Stellar gateway functionality (e.g. Coinex).

Like the other public addresses before, Stellar addresses are a string of letters and numbers of 34 digit length. Stellar addresses start with the letter "g". Stellar Exchanges may assign funds to an **individual public address** that is created newly for each registered or choose to put all funds in a **common wallet.** Individual user's funds are then accounted for by an additional **destination tag** that is added after the common wallet's public address. Exchanges may choose to assign an internal customer number or other user identifier as a destination tag.

Example of a Stellar address with destination tag (as used by some exchanges internally): gPswXyX9YqQzcdHonWK9QbGXgjGn7No1n6?dt=12345

Stellar Gateways

A list of exchanges and gateways and their public addresses is provided at the end of this book. Also a list of Stellar gateways is available from Stellar Talk [https://stellartalk.org/forum/5-gateways-exchanges/].

Like with Ripple, it is necessary to distinguish between exchanges that trade in and exchange STR (internally) and those that offer **gateway functionality** as an integrated exchange and to be integrated into the Stellar web client. Currently only **Coinex** [https://www.coinex.co.nz] and **RippleFox** [https://www.ripplefox.com] are fully functional Stellar gateways and can be **integrated** to the Stellar web client, while Kraken [https://www.kraken.com] has announced it is going to add Stellar gateway functionality "soon".

Many more **exchanges** that trade in STR, additionally to trading XRP, XBT and many other digital currencies exist but would require the **registration of an individual account**.

4 Tell me your password, again

Personal security and safety of funds is a function of the **knowledge and discretion of the user** and how he chooses to interact with and trust **other users** and **external applications**. The individual user is granted **direct control** over the execution and privacy of his financial transactions. While all transactions are published and stored in the block chain the user is not always forced surrender his identity.

Doing transactions between peers only, any intermediaries who must be trusted with data or to grant or control access can be eliminated.

High personal security therefore only requires basic knowledge about computer and internet safety and some essential understanding about how block chain based currencies and payment systems work. Becoming your own bank requires individual users to have a **minimum knowledge** of how payment processing works and adapt a certain **minimum standard for the safety** of their funds. However with respect to the security and stability of the whole system, no scale of individual action or failure can create systemic or collective risks or instability.

4.1 A psychological and behavioral problem

It is a larger psychological and behavioral problem the **average user** of digital currencies is facing. Users have long **"been conditioned"** and have learned to behave as if digital currency (or coupons and gift cards and frequent flyer points) **are not money** and has no or less value than the real money they were first acquired with.[48]

Otherwise healthy distrust and carefulness in dealing with real

---

[48] To a certain extent that is very true as various coupons and gift cards feature limited convertibility (often cannot be returned for their full nominal value) and expire at within rather short time frame. However it does not apply to block chain based currencies.

money and real persons are **safety barriers** which prevent the users from **doing stupid things**. Yet it seems if real money was exchanged for something **"less real"** or virtual and in dealing with persons over the internet many of those important barriers are torn down. **Persons spend money more easily on the internet and trust other persons more quickly**. After they have been scammed or the risk of the investment reveals itself in its entirety, users feel puzzled about their own behavior and how they could allow themselves to be cheated that easily.

Every user must understand that when choosing to trade in digital currencies (handing over money that is indeed very real), handing it over to third parties (exchanges) or revealing sensitive data about oneself to strangers - things we normally wouldn't do in "real life" with "real money" - there is a **possibility of deceit, underestimating risk, underestimating value, misjudging situations** and resulting thereof: **total loss**.

4.2 Custodial Accounts and the Unfaithful Steward

In the traditional banking environment every customer account is a **custodial account**. The bank controls the all user's funds entirely. Any bank statement or online banking display or print out is an IOU and a promise by the bank nothing more. Unless the user holds a safety deposit box with cash or other valuables in it, all bank accounts are a centrally dependent and basically a **promise up on the honor of the banks** managers.

Block chain based digital currencies give **full financial control to the user** (and owner). The user can decide to trust online wallets and / or accounts at exchanges to hold his digital funds for him or **leave the currency offline under his full control**. When funds are transferred to the custody of a third party (custodial account, exchange, online storage, etc.) they are **no longer protected by the block chain**. It is assumed that the user is fully **aware of the implications of his decision for the safety and security of his**

funds.

While most exchanges promise **an audited 100% reserve of funds** and publish audit results openly many of them are currently not subject regulatory requirements as for example the traditional banks are. Security, capital adequacy and **access control are entirely in the hands of the exchange operator,** while at the same time funds deposited with an exchange are also outside the Bitcoin security model.

A prominent failure in this respect was the **Mt. Gox exchange which had full custodial rights** over the Bitcoins deposited with it, which resulted in a disaster. Funds were stolen from Mt. Gox and or lost due to **inadequate safety and security** at that particular exchange (or due to **mismanagement**).[49]

On the other end of the spectrum the Norwegian **Justcoin exchange** was forced to stop operating as the Norwegian bank DNB refused to provide further banking services and thereby allow deposits to the exchange. Justcoin announced its orderly closure and **all its customers were able to withdraw all of their funds**. Has any bank closure in the traditional system ever been **conducted so frictionless and without damage** to users funds?

Since Mt. Gox, exchanges have improved on their internal procedures and security measures, many of them now employ hybrid models or **sophisticated security measures** like 2FA that reduce the likelihood of the user's security or that of the exchange being compromised at the same time. It is however **generally not advisable** for users to chose to **leave their funds in any (central) place** but rather in the block chain (or if exists in the native client).

---

[49] funny fact: Mt. Gox was originally founded by the later co-founder of Ripple, who subsequently went on to found Stellar.

4.3 Lack of deposit insurance / consumer protection

Why and how is a normal bank deposit insured? In many traditional banking systems customer **deposits are insured** (up to a certain amount) against bank failure. Banks fail because their **mangers make wrong investment decisions** and because they cannot payout all deposits at the same time when customers demand so.

Looking at block chain currencies demands for deposit insurance simply makes no sense. The **block chain cannot rent out your money** in bad loans and go bankrupt. Exchanges can go bankrupt but then again they **are only used for exchanging** and using a wallet at an exchange as **long term storage of your funds offers no benefits** compared to storing them **more safely under your public address, and keeping your keys in your personal storage** (desktop wallet, paper wallet, hardware wallet, native client, etc.). The Cointelegraph has recently compared hardware Bitcoin wallet solutions.[50]

Regulating exchanges to require them to take out deposit insurances seems disproportional since **most exchanges** in order to establish trust with their users have already **established a voluntary 100% reserve** requirement that most often is regularly **audited by external third parties**. Which traditional bank fulfills such high standards?

Traditional **customer protection** measures are geared against misinformation and the **resulting overselling and defrauding** of customers in the traditional financial institutions **by the traditional financial institutions** themselves and therefore make only limited sense in an industry that has **yet to proof** whether it is capable of **treating its own customers in such ways**.

Ever heard about a bank that is part of the traditional system and had

---

[50] http://cointelegraph.com/news/112947/who-will-keep-you-safe-a-comparison-of-bitcoin-wallets-that-arent-digital

to **close down and none of its customers was getting hurt**
(financially)? The Justcoin exchange closed down in November 2014
very orderly and reimbursed all its customers deposits at 100%. This
was only possible because the exchange **kept a 100% reserve** on its
deposits, **no normal bank can do or is doing that**. When normal
banks close down most customers lose at least part of their deposits.

The traditional system does not insure the customer or provides
reimbursement if the customer **transfers his funds voluntarily** to
third parties that have tricked him.[51] Yet in the discussion of the
merits and properties of block chain based currencies proponents of
the legacy systems **argue as if such kind of protection would exist**
and be the standard in the traditional banking sector (trying to make
the point that for example Bitcoin is inherently less safe). The
opposite is actually true.

When for example Ms. Haymond (Master Card) is arguing against
Bitcoins (and its cost-efficiency) she is missing the point:[52] "To
Senator Ringuette's point earlier, **yes, there are fewer fees
associated with these** [Bitcoin transfers] right now, but there are
also fewer protections. If you regulate this — this is just my own

---

[51] In a recent court case a plaintiff sued her bank to refund the money she lost
using an electronic PIN/TAN system for online transfer (the system was
penetrated by third party, man in the middle attack). The court dismissed the case
as the woman did not properly check the TAN generator display when she
authorized the transfer to an account other than she wanted to transfer her funds
to. The court argued she transferred the funds voluntarily to the wrong address for
which the bank is not liable (the customer violated her obligation to exercise due
diligence).
Urteil des LG Darmstadt (Germany), 28.08.2014 - 28 O 36/14:
[http://openjur.de/u/721428.html] and [http://dejure.org/2014,23418]
[52] Unauthorized, but contextually faithful translation by the author. Original
statement to be found at: THE STANDING SENATE COMMITTEE ON
BANKING, TRADE AND COMMERCE, OTTAWA, Issue 14 - Evidence -
October 1, 2014,
[http://www.parl.gc.ca/content/sen/committee/412/BANC/14EV-51603-
E.HTM]

personal opinion; I'm not speaking for MasterCard here — what I guess would happen is that there would be more fees associated with them, again, making it sort of a less attractive option to the underbelly, to the criminal element, and also to **entities that are looking for a cheap, no-frills solution**. I don't think there should be a cheap, no frill solution. **I think there should be consumer protection, even if that comes at some cost.**"

The **best customer protection is knowledge** of how the system works. The card industries motivation for **connecting Bitcoins with criminal activities** is to ask the legislative to **dispose of a more efficient and less costly competitor** by means of regulation. While in the case of a **near monopoly** the two major credit card companies **are all for free choice** ("no one [merchant] is forced to accept any particular credit card brand") in the case of a new technology that potentially threatens the credit cards market "**entities that are looking for a cheap, no-frills solution**" are equated with criminals. While this was only a private opinion, the argument itself reveals a lot about those working for the credit card industry: **cost-efficiency** does not seem to offer any benefit to the industry and its customers.

Critics of Bitcoin as a currency also often highlight its **unregulated nature** and **high fluctuation** as the major disadvantages and risk. Bitcoins are no legal tender and certain jurisdiction might try to ban its use. Bitcoins are not widely accepted by regular (on the street) merchants. The **few retailers that accept Bitcoin** don't keep them, but instead they chose to directly convert them to USD or EUR - they are using **Bitcoin a payment processor**.

"**Money does not have to be created legal tender** by governments. Like law, language and morals, it can emerge spontaneously. Such **private money has often been preferred to government money**, but government has usually soon suppressed it"[53] F. A. Hayek

Yes, certain governments have in the past and are currently contemplating **regulation of Bitcoin** and other protocols. Yet any attempt at regulation as a **suppression will likely prove futile**. How to suppress a technology that is **better then everything else currently available**? How to outlaw something that **works decentralized, internationally** and peer to peer? Unless we chose to abandon the internet and any other form of networking computers, **no government can stop this currency revolution**.

Also certain users joined the "Bitcoin hype" on having heard stories of "Millionaire by Christmas" but in the end saw their **investment depreciate unexpectedly**. Fact is that during the **phase of early adoption** (as is the case with new companies' stock) prices fluctuate greatly. Bitcoin and other block chain based currencies were a **very fluctuating investment**. Who is to blame if a customer **believes in infinite growth**?

4.4 In Bitcoin, the user is the weakest link

It is the **user's responsibility** to make sure the address he is sending to is right and the receiving person can be trusted to fulfill the contract, deliver the goods and services that payment was rendered on. If goods and services were not delivered as promised only **legal recourse** would exist in directly suing for **breach of contract** or informing the respective law enforcement branch of **fraud**.

Within the security model of block chain based protocols **the user** becomes and **represents the weakest link** and **greatest risk** to his own funds. No proper personal security and uninformed (misinformed) investment decisions can "wipe out" any users

---

[53] F.A. Hayek, Choice in Currency: A Way to Stop Inflation, Based on an Address entitled 'International Money' delivered to the Geneva Gold and Monetary Conference on 25 September, 1975, at Lausanne, Switzerland. IEA 1976; Mises institute/IEA 2009 [http://mises.org/page/1480]

account (faster than sending e-mail). But even in the legacy that has always been in the case. **Personal security** (known as customer protection in the traditional system) is a function of the **knowledge and discretion of the user** and how he chooses to interact with and trust other users and external applications.

Safe and sound usage of the internet and computer / mobile phones becomes an important skill. The individual user is granted direct control over the execution and privacy (and to a certain extent profitability) of his financial transactions.

High personal security therefore only requires **basic knowledge about computer and internet safety** and some essential understanding about how block chain based currencies and payment systems work.

4.5 General safety measures

As sending funds becomes as easy as sending e-mails it becomes ever more important that **safe passwords** are chosen[54]. Passwords should **not be stored locally or allowed to be automatically inserted** by the browser as this would allow anyone with access to a personal computer to **also access personal funds**.

Even before talking browser and local password storage, the **device itself** (personal computer, mobile device) must be **password protected** itself and if feasible **fully encrypted** to prevent unauthorized access if lost or stolen physically.

Some online clients and exchanges offer options for **password recovery**. Password recovery would **allow unauthorized access** if the recovery code is **sent to e-mail accounts** or devices that have been stolen or penetrated (because the e-mail password was too weak). E-mail accounts and mobile devices must therefore be

---

[54] A list of password generators is provided in the resources chapter, use at your own risk.

properly guarded and protected.

Where possible and offered, the user should make use of **two factor verification procedures** that only grant access to funds when additional one time use passwords are provided through another channel (e.g. mobile phone).

Criminals know they **cannot possibly hack the block chain protocol,** so they will go after the weakest link in the user's personal security (e.g. weak e-mail passwords).

Be careful what you click, online and in email. If you don't trust the site or the person that sent you a link, don't click it. **Up-to-date antivirus** can help protect you against malicious software (malware) that may attempt to steal your account details and other sensitive data. Malware and potentially unwanted programs are increasingly distributed (as additional / silent install) with other free software.

4.6 Redirect and Phishing

User log-in data and passwords are **easily compromised through phishing** attacks or sites that pretend to be the original (e.g. exchange / web client) login site.

Malicious websites may pretend to be your exchange / web client or ask you to recover you **login details that "were lost"** in order to obtain your account information and password and retain access. Such attacks also may come in the form of invitations to claim **"wins" or "inheritance"** from far relatives and even completely unknown persons or to share **"orphaned accounts"** worth millions.

Think twice before clicking on links that promise **"free money"** you might lose all as a result. Just because **a "phisher" may know your name or log-in already** doesn't mean that they're legitimate.

To **enter any of your information** into any site that is not the genuine client **is to give away access to your funds**. Users should only login to websites and domains that are **"spelled properly"** and are showing the **secure access** web protocol "https" in the browser address bar.

Phishing can be compared to an unknown person on the street asking you to give him all your account data and login. Would you do that in real life?

5 No just a superior currency and payment processing

Why are block chain based digital currencies **superior to traditional currencies** and how payments are processed? What block chain based currencies **can do and the Dollar or Euro cannot**? The following chapter discusses **properties and issues** of block chain based currencies and payment processing **compared with the legacy system**. My discussion is largely based on the testimony of Mr. Antonopoulos before the Canadian Senate[55] and to lesser extent on Mr. Brown's "Thoughts on the future of finance".

5.1 Push versus Pull procedures = control and freedom versus trust and counterparty risk

Bitcoin is all about **building a trust-free decentralized transaction register** (the block chain): "[...] The whole point of Bitcoins is that they are **counterparty-risk-free** assets: my Bitcoin is not somebody else's liability." Mr. Brown, IBM UK[56]

By contrast, Ripple (and Stellar) are all about dealing with assets that are **somebody else's liability**. Like in our current financial system we are dealing with trust and resulting risks. The focus of Ripple and Stellar is therefore on representing liabilities issued **by identifiable issuers** (exchanges, gateways) and enabling trade on a network by **granting control** over how much we trust a certain issuer. Issuers need to be trusted before any trade can happen.

This **control over whom we trust** and how much is an **essential freedom**. This freedom is not granted to the user of the traditional banking system.

---

[55] Senate Testimony of Mr. Antonopoulos, source see above
[56] Richard Gendal Brown, Ripple is hard to understand, but it's worth making the effort: there's a deep insight at its core, at his blog "Thoughts on the future of finance" [http://gendal.wordpress.com/category/ripple/]

The (Bitcoin) block chain can **account for Bitcoins only** while **Ripple** (and Stellar) **can move any kind** of stored value or asset (including Bitcoin IOUs). While the native unit of accounting (e.g. XRP or STR) is traded against other currencies and assets the **user does not need to buy it in order to move funds.** Users of Ripple and Stellar can altogether **avoid the risk of the (native) currencies' fluctuation.**

"By contrast, a user needs to buy bitcoins to access the blockchain, and be exposed to the volatility inherent in a bitcoin purchase."[57]

In the **traditional banking system** with initiating a onetime deposit, transfer or withdrawal most often users also **give implicit consent** not only to the loss of mentioned freedom but also to the loss of individual security.

Mr. Antonopoulos[58] describes this as the difference of **security and risk in (decentralized) push and (centralized) pull systems**: In using digital currencies it is important to understand that they are actually more like independent units of exchange (i.e. cash, commodities, gold) as opposed to giro money (the money on your bank account) debit and credit cards.

The "push" mechanism in the Bitcoin protocol **transfers value directly** in the form of a token of value (the Bitcoin's / XBT), while credit, debit and giro "pull" from an account that the user is authorized to access by an authority or clearinghouse.

"This concept of **disintermediation, or removing intermediaries** and connecting directly buyers to sellers, lenders to creditors and consumers to merchants, without intermediaries, is **the magical power of bitcoin**. That's what this invention has allowed us to do,

---

[57] Patrick Griffin, Executive Vice President of Business Development at Ripple Labs [http://bankinnovation.net/2014/10/ripple-ecosystem-expands-with-british-startup-ripula/]
[58] Senate Testimony of Mr. Antonopoulos, source see above

without having to establish trust first." [59] Mr. Antonopoulos

One of the big failures of regulation in the legacy system is that with centralized identifiers and centralized regulation comes **centralization of risk**. So when an organization or institution is hacked, and loses millions of customer identities that has direct impact on those millions of users. Foremost the user needs to consider that such failures, leaks and the (subsequent) sale of private data can **only happen because those institutions were storing those millions of user identities in the first place**.

"So the advantage of a decentralized environment is that **there is no central repository**, motherlode, cache, vault where everyone's identity is stored and, therefore, everyone's identity can [can't] be attacked at the same time." [60] Mr. Antonopoulos

In the case of Bitcoin and other digital currencies no prior (and standing) **authorization** is necessary. A onetime "push" **does not expose sensitive data** or grants rights of continuous withdrawal. Every **transfer is authorized by the user only** and in return holds no risk for the receiving party as it **cannot be reversed or charged back**[61] Charge backs offer no additional security to the customer as in most cases of fraud and scam the money is most likely gone anyway.

Likewise there is **no counterparty** risk in Ripple and Stellar. But both currencies' worth lies more in their payment protocol that enables the transfer of any kind of asset. The internal unit of accounting (XRP/ STR) is rather **risk free** (not regarding volatility) but what is transferred through the payment system are the liabilities (IOUs) of a certain issuer, which certainly may hold a high risk depending on each individual type of IOU and the issuer itself.

---

[59] Senate Testimony of Mr. Antonopoulos, source see above
[60] Senate Testimony of Mr. Antonopoulos, source see above
[61] Senate Testimony of Mr. Antonopoulos, source see above

5.2 Security and inherent stability

According to Mr. Antonopoulos, the **fundamental design flaw of the legacy system** is centralization and tying identity to every transaction and thereby creating **systems that can continuously draw from the users' accounts**. Bitcoin is fundamentally different, it reveals no information that directly indentifies the user (only the user's public address, that is a pseudonym). For every digital currency and payment system users may take steps to further strengthen their privacy, **the flow of money** is however **always transparent**. Thereby many block chain based currencies constitute a safe haven for the users' identity but not a place for money to hide.

Under the impression of various leaks and security breaches in the legacy systems of traditional banking and payment processing, it is the a simple conclusion that **consumers cannot be better protected by removing their ability to control their own privacy** and then forcing them to entrust it in intermediaries (that have failed them so many times before).

The European Banking Authority (EBA) has published a lengthy opinion on the use of virtual currencies[62] and the **potential dangers** therein in August 2014.[63] Main concerns voiced are related to the **risk of total investment loss**, high volatility and possible scams, predominantly however repeat long known **issues of doing business on the internet**. As the new currencies enable the transfer of money at the ease of sending e-mail basic **security measures and sound and safe behavior** on the net become indispensible traits for the general user.

---

[62] Which throws all existing digital currencies into the same category of "virtual currencies" and discusses possible problems and risks only on a very general basis. The advantages of established first generation block chain based currencies and their (second and third generation) successors for example to the safety and security of payment processing are altogether ignored.
[63] [www.eba.europa.eu/documents/10180/657547/EBA-Op-2014-08+Opinion+on+Virtual+Currencies.pdf]

It should be a "no-brainer" to **choose strong passwords** and not to give your e-mail access away to unknown persons. Yet with respect to the new payment possibilities some users are rather harshly confronted with how **inherently unsafe** their otherwise **normal internet usage** and routine behavior is.[64]

Risk is compartmentalized through networking independent and equal participants and through a decentralized and distributed payment verification. There is no central bank or authority and **no concentration of power** in the hands of payment processors or banks. Within Bitcoin there are no institutions that could become so systemic relevant they can bring down the whole system. **No single participant in the network is irreplaceable**, so there is **no risk** based on the centralization of authority or user information and the possible compromise of such.

That however does not mean there is no individual security risk. Before the Canadian Senate Banking Committee, Mr Antonopoulos described the situation in simple words: "**Individual Bitcoin wallets**, my wallet **can be hacked**, and we see examples of that. **The system as a whole cannot be hacked**."[65] For a moment consider anyone made a similar statement with regard to the legacy system.

In Bitcoin there will never be a wholesale leak or sale of user access data (the private keys). **Each account must be "broken in" individually** thereby making such attacks economically less plausible.

Noone would leave his front door open while having a Million Dollar laying on the kitchen table. Similarly leaving the door to your personal bank vault wide open (by not choosing strong passwords) is

---

[64] The limits and dangers of not knowing what we do as individuals and what macro-economic and environmental consequences actually will result from our collective actions and in-action have been demonstrated in our shared economic and environmental history. Here however personal routine and normal behavior (if not also safe) carries direct personal and financial risks.
[65] Senate Testimony of Mr. Antonopoulos, source see above

a invitation to theft.

While **individual network nodes might be taken over** and release wrong information there is **no permanent effect to the integrity** of a distributed, decentralized network where entries into the common ledger are decided by the **consensus of the nodes**.[66] This is not to be misinterpreted – it is not the community (other users) but protocol nodes that witness and verify automatically all transactions.

Whereas (in the traditional system) if a culprit brakes into a credit card company or the database of a major retailer **who stores credit card information centrally**, this information can be used almost immediately to cause **direct financial harm** to the respective account holders.[67]

As there is **no such central point that could be attacked** in (decentralized) block chain based currencies, no information that would grant access to funds and could harm users can ever be leaked, sold or stolen directly from the underlying payment processing system.

That fact alone makes block chain based currencies **safer than any other currency and payment processing system in place today**.[68] What is the case for any other complex procedure and system likewise holds true for block chain based currencies: individual safety and security will always depend on the knowledge, choice and actions of the user.

---

[66] The cost of a "51% attack" (to "out-compute" all honest nodes) is currently estimated at about USD 613 171 600, which would fool the system for 10 minutes. Subsequently one hour of this kind of attack would cost around USD 3 682 296 000. (There are currently USD 1.29 trillion in circulation)

[67] Mann, Ian, Hacking the human: social engineering techniques and security countermeasures, Gower Publishing, 2008, ISBN: 978-0-566-08773-8

[68] Just consider that 40% of Visa cards business is fraud prevention and fraud case management. Imagine an equal percentage of costs being unnecessary.

5.3 Cut out the middleman and limit third party interference

Undoubtedly the use value of Ripple and Stellar as a **payment protocol** is higher than that of the Bitcoin protocol, simply for **transactions being verified more quickly** and for offering an **integrated exchange function** and **not requiring the user to buy and hold** initially and potentially fluctuating currency and **internal unit of account**. As **a store of value token** Bitcoin seems **more robust and longer tested**.

The **business case** for block chain based currencies is in general that they allow companies and individuals alike to cut the banks and any other intermediary out of the loop. Specifically those digital currencies and payment protocols allow businesses and individuals alike to **save high fees and commission** which are rendered on a slow and low level service – that is the simple accounting and transfer of numbers from one account to the other.

Bitcoins cannot be inflated, no government can control a network of peers or could force them to mine and supply more. The causes for currency **inflation and devaluation are directly limited**, essentially robbing governments of their ability to **raise money by printing it**.

Certainly one can calculate the inflationary effect of the Bitcoins based on the issuance of the mining reward. However the demand for Bitcoins is much higher, creating a greater deflationary effect. Mr Antonoupolus calls it "a **persistant deliberate deflationary effect**" that is built into the [Bitcoin] currency.[69]

Being deprived of the ability to inflate "their" **national currency** governments would find it **difficult to pay for expensive long term foreign engagements** (i.e. wars). **Saving money and preventing wars** (making them more difficult to finance) – can it get any better?

---

[69] Bitcoin Cryptocurrency Crash Course with Andreas Antonopoulos - Jefferson Club Dinner Meetup [http://www.youtube.com/watch?v=JP9-lAYngi4]

5.4 Access and public auditing

The Bitcoin protocol is **open for business every hour** of the day and knows no holidays. In its openness the Bitcoin network surpasses even it own foundation, the internet (for its delivery the consumer usual has to pay a provider). Also its source code is openly available, which has important implications for its **safety and the trust users extend to it**.

Once vulnerabilities (and loopholes) are known, security experts and developers have the choice to immediately and fully disclose the risk and thereby enable the users to take preventive actions by themselves. However such **immediate and full information disclosure** about possible risks might not reach every user in time and in itself entails the risk of also informing possible "hackers" of open vulnerabilities.

Most digital currencies and payment protocols based on the block chain technology are open source, which means the code of their software is disclosed publicly and **allows every developer and user to audit the safety** and stability of the respective system.[70] No user should ever join a payment processing system that keep its policies and procedures a secret or tells the user **"you do not need to know"**.

This enables many experts and normal users to participate in the hunt for vulnerabilities in the software and the protocol's policies thereby **eliminating many risks** before the protocol gains widespread adoption.

Another option to deal with security and stability issues is to **fix the vulnerability and quickly release updates**. The ability to fix problems however depends on knowing that A. a problem exists, B.

---

[70] As is the case with any business investment decision if there is no full disclosure the customer / user / buyer / investor should ask himself what might be the reason why the information is not fully disclosed.

having the resources and knowledge how to best fix it.

A single team of developers might not be aware of all possible exploits in their code. Also internal development teams usually command **limited resources** only to address a particular issue.

The advantage of the open source approach is that software **risks are found out quickly by a larger community** of stakeholders and possibly **get fixed more quickly** based on their input and suggestions.

Systemic safety and security of the protocol of block chain based currencies is a given right from the start when the (open) source code is audited and evaluated by experts and the public at large. If loopholes arise that evaded the eyes of so many auditors and developers those can be fixed nearly instantly through updates.

5.5 The cost of centralization and regulation

The centralization of power and authority necessitates **oversight and regulation** and most often results in **increasing the costs of economic exchange**. The security measures and **customer protection** approach of the traditional system intends to **protect the customers** from abuse through the traditional banking system itself and through increased costs **results in economic exclusion**, resistance to innovation and resistance to market entry and possible competition.

In his testimony before the Standing Senate Committee on Banking of the Canadian Parliament Mr Antonopoulos described the **disadvantages of the centralized legacy system** with very harsh words[71]: "The entities near the centre of a traditional financial network are vested with **enormous power**, act with full authority, and therefore must be **carefully investigated**, regulated and **subject**

---

[71] Senate Testimony of Mr. Antonopoulos, source see above

to oversight. Centralized financial networks can **never be fully open to innovation** because their security depends on **access control**. Incumbents in such networks effectively utilize **access control to stifle innovation and competition,** presenting it as consumer protection."[72]

Centralization also **creates fragility** as big individual actors and institutions become relevant to the **stability of the whole system**. Power concentration in those systemic relevant institutions has required **governmental intervention and bailouts**. That is the taxpayer has bailed out those institutions that stifle competition and thereby are able to impose a fee structure that is not actually based on actual costs incurred in the financial transactions themselves.

It is one lesson of the financial crisis of 2008/2009 (sub prime housing crisis / global financial crisis) that the traditional financial system's concentrated power, created cozy relationships between themselves and their regulators which led to **regulatory capture**.[73]

The regulatory capture, the market power abuse, the corruption, the intransparency and **complexity of products** offered, the **betting against those products** that were sold to institutional investors "with the highest ratings", recent **exchange rate and interest rate fixing**, etc. are just a examples of symptoms of the **systemic problems of the traditional financial institutions** and the inability or unwillingness of governments to **equally enforce the law among all social strata** of their citizens.

Digital currencies based on the **block chain technology** avoid many of the systemic and inherent pitfalls through **transparency** and a new model of **decentralized open economic exchange**.

---

[72] Senate Testimony of Mr. Antonopoulos, source see above
[73] in the case of the derivative market in the United States: the abandonment of any regulation altogether

5.6 Openness and economic inclusion

No one can be stopped from participating and sharing the benefits of block chain based currencies. The Bitcoin network is **open to anyone** to participate without vetting, without authentication, and **without prior authorization**. The network is ignorant of nationality and ethnicity and also on whether there exists a working (banking) infrastructure in the user's immediate environment or not.

The traditional banking and payment processing model relies on **centralized control**. Security is dependent on a central authority. The whole design of the traditional financial network centers on **system relevant authorities** and clearing houses with centralized security procedures. Security is administered and authority over the whole system is exercised by central institutions with **linear security procedures**.

This results in a security design that largely resembles a pyramid in its **hierarchical structure**. The problem with that financial model is that the lower categories of participants in this economic system **are not afforded complete and open access**. The further we move down this hierarchical structure the more **limited access rights** and therefore **economic participation** gets.

The basis of the pyramid, which represents the largest part of the global population, is not afforded any or **only the most basic services** and at the same time, for a lower level of access to those services, is charged with **proportionally higher fees and commissions** (cost of exchange in general).

This is a **security and economic model** that by strictly controlling access **favors exclusion** and when large parts of the society are denied access they also become **disenfranchised from economic progress**. The reason why so many populations are excluded is that the cost of bringing the legacy infrastructure to them is higher than what they could possibly pay in fees. The outdated legacy infrastructure is simply too expensive.

5.7 Global registry of property rights and economic inclusion

Modern economics is rooted in the belief that **everyone benefits from free trade** (Richardo's Theory of Comparative Advantage). Any barriers to trade are generally bad for the world economy (as a whole). That is why **economists are normally supportive** of any politics and systems that **make international trade easier**. It is a fact that Bitcoin makes (free) trade easier.

Bitcoin is the **first globally available processing system** for sending value around the world nearly instantly. Bitcoin as a payment system is a very powerful tool **supporting continued globalization of trade** - for the first time however making it transparent and **granting access to everyone on equal terms**.

"Economists that are true to their roots should recognize this opportunity." Kenny Spotz[74]

Hernando de Soto investigated **why capitalism is more successful in the West** but has generated mixed results at best in many other countries. His answer is the **lack of liquid capital** in underdeveloped economies. De Soto tracks the questions what is capital and how it is created to the **question of ownership and the (official) certification** of such as property **rights, titles and rules** of incorporation.

"The poor inhabitants of these nations—five-sixths of humanity—do **have things**, but they lack the process to **represent their property** and **create capital**. They have houses but **not titles**; crops but **not deeds**; businesses but not statutes of incorporation. It is the

---

[74] Kenny Spotz in his article on "why economists should love bitcoin" [http://cointelegraph.com/news/112813/4-reasons-why-economists-should-love-bitcoin]

64

unavailability of these essential representations that explains why people who have adapted every other Western invention, from the paper clip to the nuclear reactor, have not been able to produce sufficient capital to **make their domestic capitalism work**."[75]

Bitcoin creates a **supra-national inventory** that allows anyone to establish and access **property and business rights and titles** and so turn assets into **leverageable capital**.[76] It therefore allows the disadvantaged parts of any society to **bypass local (inefficient) governments** and inaccessible or corrupt procedures together with **instable** or "domestic-use-only" **currencies**.

The block chain technology can **transform otherwise dead capital into assets, titles and liquidity** that can be traded and leveraged. Therefore it can connect subsistence farmers to global markets by allowing them to establish and trade and contracts (**capital formation**) in otherwise **dysfunctional administrative / governmental environments**.

Disenfranchised societies anywhere in the world can (through Bitcoin and other block chain technologies) be given **access to open source, democratic, and decentralized forms of bureaucracy** and government services at minimal cost.

5.8 Leapfroging technologies – Accessing global markets

Mr. Antonopoulos describes Bitcoin as[77] "a technology that has the possibility of bringing **economic inclusion to billions** of people who do not have it today in the same way that **cell phone**

---

[75] Hernando De Soto, The Mystery of Capital: Why Capitalism Triumphs in the West and Fails Everywhere Else, Basic Books, 2003, ISBN: 978-0465016150
[76] Admittedly the procedure and system of doing (providing certifications services) so is still in its infancy as most government do not allow their established legacy notary systems to be bypassed. Yet, the possibility exists that two users can agree to certify documents between themselves on a private contract basis.

technology allowed entire nations to **leapfrog the landline** and land in a technology realm and **achieve communications** […] Bitcoin **can do the same for banking** and finance. It can **empower billions of people** around the world in areas such as remittances, international finance and credit, accessing liquidity and loans, etc."

Bitcoin and other block chain based currencies are **a low friction digital money** that can be introduced into an environment without the need for building massive infrastructure. Through wireless (phone) technologies that bring internet connection it can **introduce banking and financial services** to regions that don't have access to that service presently for **lack of any (western financial) legacy infrastructure**.

The user of the most simple smart phone can become a bank serving thousands of customers **accessing and trading on the world's markets**, communicating with lower tech (non-smart) phones **though short text** messaging.

Block chain based currencies are as if one **created a new language that everyone can understand** and can use instantly. It is connecting people. It is connecting markets. Beyond getting connected and becoming a participant, **people themselves become markets, become banks**. It allows anyone to participate no matter where they are from, what formal language they speak or how much debt their natural government has amassed. It gives entire populations control of their own finances and **direct access to an undistorted and international market**.

5.9 Transparency and law enforcement

There are some hefty misconceptions around, based on not properly understanding how the block chain protocol works and what it designed to do and enable[78].

Ms. Haymond (Master Card)[79] for example classifies Bitcoin in the following way: "This means **no consumer protections**, no disclosures, no error resolution, no dispute rights and **no lost or stolen protection**. When you consider these factors, it is apparent that part of Bitcoin's current appeal is the **inability of many law enforcement agencies to trace its transactions**, and this anonymity has made it a payment method of choice for illegal transactions […]".

To the contrary, the central public ledger allows any user to observe all transactions that occur on the network (**full disclosure, full transparency, real time**). True is that those transactions are **not tied to a specific identity** or physical address, but with the use of traditional law enforcement mechanisms, when an identity is attached to a specific transaction for example through the KYC/AML procedures at exchanges or points of withdrawal, that **transaction can be followed throughout the network**, and therefore the Bitcoin network does not afford more anonymity than for example cash or giro money.

It is a well known fact that **networking and digitalization** of information **has led to reduced levels of privacy**. In fact, it is **easier to implement strong transparency** and accountability features on a network of block chain based currencies **than it is to achieve strong anonymity**. Achieving full anonymity with Bitcoin would go beyond the knowledge and capability of the normal user.[80]

---

[78] find a full list of Bitcoin Myths at [https://en.bitcoin.it/wiki/Myths]
[79] The Standing Senate Committee on Banking, Trade and Commerce, Issue 14 - Evidence - October 1, 2014, Ottawa
[http://www.parl.gc.ca/Content/SEN/Committee/412/banc/14ev-51603-e.htm?Language=E&Parl=41&Ses=2&comm_id=3]
[80] Anonymity/deniability has also proven to be beyond the technical expertise of the operators of the illegal Silk Road 1.0 (and recently 2.0) which were all busted

Yet, even within the traditional currencies and **legacy banking procedures**, methods do exist to **conceal the origin and destination of** funds and protect the identity of the issuing and receiving parties. Companies and private persons alike (with the help of specialized firms and local governments) find it not difficult to navigate international and local law to evade taxes on a large scale.[81]

Anonymity as it is important to every user can be achieved, but far greater use value and **application potential** of block chain based currencies lies in its **transparency and traceability**. If governments and companies adopted block chain based currencies, all cooperate and public spending (conducted with it) would instantly be transparent and traceable.

The public ledger and block chain is **available openly to the public** and all law enforcement branches of any government can use it directly for **analysis in real-time without any special requirements** (technically or procedure-wise). Most western countries do have **privacy protection and banking secret laws** which requires law enforcement agencies to apply for the release of private information when dealing with traditional banks.

"Know Your Customer" and "Anti-Money-Laundering" are already enforced on most exchanges. However traditional and in most times **paper based information systems require time** and in many cases dictate an exact procedure to be followed. Concerning Bitcoin anyone can use tools like the block chain explorer [https://blockchain.info/] and explore his own or other public addresses.

"As with any technology, this **technology will reflect society**, and there will be a tiny minority that will try to use it for evil. But I have

---

for selling drugs and other contra-band by the United States FBI applying rather traditional law enforcement procedures.
[81] [http://online.wsj.com/articles/luxembourg-tax-leak-puts-eus-juncker-under-further-pressure-1415276250]

full faith that **law enforcement capabilities** properly exercised can follow funds on Bitcoin just as they can in the normal financial networks probably more so than they can in traditional financial networks."[82] Mr. Antonopoulos

5.10 Real money after all?

Only bits and bytes on a computer - can it really be the future money?

Bitcoin and other digital currencies fulfill the **requirements to and properties of money**, which are commonly described as scarcity, durability, divisibility, fungibility, recognisability.

Bitcoin is **governed by the mathematical algorithms** in its source code. Those algorithms offer the user **predictable results and objectivity** as opposed to political motivated financial and monetary decisions. No government can decide to print or mint more Bitcoins (and so cause inflation) as it is not in their hands. The current formula limits the total number of Bitcoins to a maximum of **21 million to be created** until the year 2140.

Furthermore what could be described as the banks of the new system, the exchanges have almost exclusively adopted a 100% reserve standard and submitted themselves to **external auditing and proof of funds procedures**. In comparison the central banks' promise to bail out failing commercial banks is based on the government's authority to print more money, and thereby devalue it.

While Bitcoin is guaranteed to be scarce (**scarcity**), other digital currencies (e.g. Stellar) might introduce an easier money supply in order to avoid hoarding of the tokens and units of accounting. What all block chain based currencies have in common is that the common ledger is **redundantly backed up** on thousands of computers and

---

[82] Senate Testimony of Mr. Antonopoulos, source see above

every user can back up his or her public and private keys to their Bitcoins in many different safe ways, making them a **very durable and resilient** asset (**durability**). Bitcoin, Ripple and Stellar are highly **divisible** (up to 10^{-8})[83].

Digital currencies in general are extremely **easy and fast to transfer** - also internationally (**fungibility**). **Verification for authenticity** takes place almost instantly and a **high encryption** rate makes the modern block chain based digital currencies **virtually unforgeable** (**recognisability**).

Those properties make it possible that money (that the modern block chain based digital currencies) may serve as

- **medium of exchange and a**

- **unit of account and**

- **to store value.**

The **portability** of traditional money has made it an **easy target for theft**. Digital currencies are **not exempt from that problem**. Where however long term storage of traditional money might **not be beneficial** if governments decide to print more of it, a digital currency like Bitcoin offers a real alternative as it does stand **outside the traditional system** of government controlled **monetary policy**.

One might argue that Bitcoins have **no intrinsic value**[84], but that is

---

[83] 21 million Bitcoins can be created until the year 2140. Each being divisible until 10^{-8} yields a theoretical total of 2,099,999,997,690,000 exchangeable units and value tokens. Approximately 100 times the number of red blood cells in the human body.
[84] Alan Greenspan did so, but then again that is perfectly natural for a former head of the Federal Reserve Bank of the United States. It would not occur to such a functionary to allow theorising about private money that would render the institution he once headed obsolete. Though he admits that the quantitative easing policy introduced under his chairmanship has failed, stopping it will have potentially destabilising effects. In other words the policy that was introduced and is till followed is openly labelled to be wrong (as has bad side effects) but it cannot

a property they do share with their government issued counterparts. Coins and **paper money are easy to print and mint**. The value of the raw materials they are made of is (in the normal case) incomparably small compared to the value they nominally represent and store. **Giro money of any currency holds even lower intrinsic value** as it is just like like Bitcoins only bits and bytes on a computer. The difference is **Bitcoins are encrypted** and therefore cannot be created out of nothing, like for example the traditional banks create and give credit (giro money and loans). Being encrypted Bitcoins are **intrinsically more secure and safe**.

The block chain does not give credit, nor does it loan out the user's money. The user may consent to loan out his money or supply his Bitcoins as the basis for **fractional reserve banking**, such business is however only possible with the users explicit consent and not part of the Bitcoin protocol. Most exchanges of the block chain based currencies have until noe not seen any benefit in introducing fractional reserves but continue to hold full reserves on their customers' deposits.

The **perceived and accepted value** of most government issued money **bases on the collective belief** that it can always be exchanged for its face value and that this value is protected and relatively stable.[85] **The government creates and protects** national (and in the case of the Euro - supra-national) currency by **declaring it legal tender** and sometimes outlawing other currencies as possible means of alternative tender. The government establishes demand for its own currency by **legal force**. In fact the government **establishes a monopoly**. The general public and companies accept the national currencies as it is the **only way to pay taxes** and settle public

---

be stopped because of potentially stronger repercussion that would follow (i.e. because we do not know what to do else).

[85] This belief is not always justified, but often was shattered very easily. Few governments have been proven able to artificially lower or raise the exchange rate of their free floating national currencies if such manipulation was not backed by a substantial economic power.

debts.[86]

Despite fulfilling the required properties of money, **digital currencies are not currently government approved** or regulated legal tender. As with other kinds of private money each individual or merchant has the right to accept or not to accept a digital currency unless a government introduces regulation to the contrary.

"The government attempts to guard the value of money by maintaining a monopoly on its production to avoid counterfeiting, and by establishing a central bank with a mandate to manage its supply **responsibly over time**.

[..] this relationship amongst government, central bank, households, corporates and fiat currencies is much more efficient than an alternative like barter. It also makes **macroeconomic shocks much easier to manage** than an alternative like the gold standard (recall the deflation of the Great Depression and more recently peripheral Europe)"[87] John Normand, JP Morgan

Here exactly lies one promise of the digital currency revolution. **Recalling** "peripheral Europe" and **remembering** that recent "macroeconomic shocks" actually did have their origin in the **actions of governments in collaboration with the established financial institutions**, taking this high responsibility of financial and monetary and policy out of their hands by establishing and **imposing financial discipline on governments, households and companies alike** seems a necessary step. Given the solidity of block chain based digital currencies it is also **a practical option.**

---

[86] It is not unheard of that in times of crisis however governments have preferred to accept commodities instead of their own legal tender.
[87] John Normand, JP Morgan, Global Rates & FX Research, 11 February 2014, "The audacity of bitcoin: Risks and opportunities for corporates and investors" (GPS-1319815-0)
[https://docs.google.com/file/d/0B0xHDZkxOzjMc0cwZFlqbGd4RzJNWkZldk p5QzBYUWFOTUhr/edit?pli=1]

Digital currencies can introduce a system based on a totally fixed or slow-growing money supply (the example of Bitcoin), but are also flexible enough to introduce a modest level of continual inflation (in the case of Stellar) to **encourage spending over hoarding**.

5.11 Infinity on a finite planet

Most modern democracies suffer from the flaw that what makes sense politically is often **a terrible idea economically**. Governments resort to **printing money to finance their political ambitions**. The problem with printing money is that it corrupts the persons and countries that do it.

Inflation is just an outwardly appearance of it, the ability to wage costly wars simply another by-product. The major issue is that the **power to inflate a currency creates the illusion of infinity of available resources** on a finite planet. Prices are there to reflect scarcity.

Political choices and democratic decision making get obfuscated; **wrong priorities are set and followed**. Governments postpone painful choices and **disregard natural economic limitations** and social necessities alike.

Whoever just mentions harsh realities and limitations does not get voted. He who **promises ever rising wages and dividends**, or just keeps a **broken and predatory system** running a little longer is elevated to the highest offices. Growth and success sells, conservation and restraint are no topics to win an election with.

8% of the US GDP is financial services which brings it very close to the **ancient system of tithe** (i.e. tenth part duty being paied to the roman catholic church) and according to Mr. Antonopoulos is evidence for the widespread inefficiency of this service industry today (if the money movement was more efficient it share in the GDP wouldn't be that high).

If any government is allowed to **manipulate its money supply** it will do so **for a political reasoning** that normally has nothing to do with sound economics. **Separating politics from economic decisions** will ultimately bring more stability to both areas.

"**We don't need a central bank or governmental authority** to tell us something is legal tender or to say it has **legal based legitimacy**. Bitcoin is a demonstration in **market based legitimacy**. This alone has **profound implications for society**, for financial services, and also for interactions with respect to digital assets going into the future that we can't even comprehend yet."[88] Jon W. Mantonis, Head of the Bitcoin Foundation

Likewise F. A. Hayek insisted that "the free market is the only mechanism that has ever been discovered for achieving **participatory democracy**."[89]

5.12 Speculation and widespread adoption

Many **users and investors** in digital currencies can **see and understand the philosophical and political character** of the decentralized digital currencies while mostly **taking advantage of their practical use** (e.g. easy, cheap and fast money transfer). Not few are compelled by the idea of speculation for easy profit and it cannot be denied that there is **much speculation going on in the new virtual currencies** which results in a high price fluctuation.

Price fluctuation (exchange rate fluctuation) in Bitcoins and other digital currencies is in part caused by unreasonable expectation and respective **speculative investment activity**. Price fluctuation remains one of the bigger caveats. For several observers and proponents of Bitcoins as a currency however it is a given that

---

[88] [http://cointelegraph.com/news/112813/4-reasons-why-economists-should-love-bitcoin]
[89] F.A. Hayek, Collected Works, Vol. 2: The Road to Serfdom, p 260

liquidity will improve and we will eventually see **more stable exchange rates** which will in turn encourage Bitcoins **wider adoption** as an alternative (international) currency.

However logic such argument may sound it is obviously a **circular argument**. First the liquidity is going up, then exchange rates stabilize, from which **widespread adoption** follows, which actually would be the major reason and **prerequisite for the liquidity** to improve in the first place

"Whether or not **crypto-currencies** are **superior than today's currencies** for today's payment problems isn't really interesting. It's like saying that the automobile is a terrible way of pulling a plough. Crypto-currency technology will succeed only to the extent that **it enables new products and services** that were previously impossible or unimaginable." Richard Brown, IBM UK[90]

Traditional currencies are just money, they lack payment processing. Bitcoin and others are **currencies and payment processing in one**. And in the combination of both are ultimately much more.

A very convincing argument for widespread adoption of Bitcoin is that it enables **use cases and scenarios that are inconceivable with "normal currency"** and in the traditional system. New applications **will drive the adoption of Bitcoins and other digital currencies**. As the underlying protocol enables previously unimaginable applications (products and services) the **native currency of the protocol becomes the natural choice** for any transfer between the users of those products and services.

5.13 Next-generation use cases

One of the **next-generation use cases** (non-money use cases) proposed for the block chain is that of a **notary,** to register property

---

[90] [http://gendal.wordpress.com/2014/10/05/cryptocurrency-products-and-services-will-determine-adoption-of-the-currency-not-the-other-way-round/]

and certify documents. Instead of relying on a central authority the authenticity of a document or contract can be verified through block chain technology. The decentralized ledger is used as an impartial public record for it provides time stamping and user verification for all sorts of things (from bicycles to cars, company shares and even marriages).[91]

With the registration of the smallest fraction of a Bitcoin **two users can register and transfer titles** and deeds and use and service contracts for any kind of property.

Real-world relationships and **contracts can often be reduced to deterministic rules** that can be executed by a neutral, unimpeachable platform. And these contracts often (not always) involve the **exchange of economic value**, usually in the form of the native currency of the platform.

"Even better and more importantly, **the car could look up its own title and render itself usable to the new owner** automatically. This concept is called **smart property**, where the property recognizes its ownership through reference to the blockchain."[92] Mr. Antonopoulus

In the **economy of things and internet of things** devices can discover, connect and collaborate. Devices and applications can also pay each other for **access to resources and information**.

Upon submitting a transaction on the block chain with a smart phone that phone can **unlock doors** to apartments, hotel rooms or allow

---

[91] Here we are back at the question posed by Reverend Johann Friedrich Zöllner and Johann Erich Biester
"Proposal, not to engage the clergy any longer when marriages are conducted" (in the Berlinische Monatsschrift , April 1783) that triggered Kant's famous response. But our question takes the issue to a completely new level: Should the government still be bothered when marriages are conducted? or isn't a completely private matter that can be certified / notarized via time stamping through a block chain?
[92] Senate Testimony of Mr. Antonopoulos, source see above

you access **any other kind of property**.

CoinPrism / ChromaWallet can be used to **issue a company's stock on the blockchain** so that it can be traded and transferred without the need of all surrounding and additional procedure we apply to traditional stock trading. This use-case has nothing to do with currency. The Bitcoins are **just being used as a transport layer**. The Bitcoin scripting system allows users to make binding bids and offers **without needing a central exchange**.

Having a currency and payment protocol in one that can be programmed (scripting) allows the possibility of **automating all kinds of financial transactions** even complicated and international ones. The introduction of such a technology is equivalent to the introduction of the steam and the combustion engine or electricity to industrial production. Surely it will not only disrupt those businesses that have insisted on keeping their horses for too long but it will also create whole new economies and industrial branches.

Block chain based technology allows **innovation of products and services** as the internet has done before. Therefore this book has gone as far as claiming this technology presents all qualities necessary to **start a new industrial and socio-economic revolution**.

6 Conclusion - Why economists hate Bitcoin and why it does not matter

Peter Šurda comments on "Why economists hate Bitcoin":[93] "Bitcoin **exposes a lot of fallacies in the assumptions** (implicit or explicit) that economists make. The function of media of exchange, the function of money, the conflict between the goals of banks (commercial and central) and the "consumers" of our monetary system, and so on. This causes cognitive dissonance. **People do not like to confront the idea that they have been wrong for years**."

Utopian, dystopian or completely improbable the user and customer decides, the future will show. The new digital currencies are no financial product of the Bank elites and also do not spring from universities nor grand economic theories. Bitcoin originates and is carried by the mainstream of society as a proof of market-based legitimacy.

We **do not need those** unfaithful stewards, nor economists, academics or **financial professionals** telling us what is the best solution. We can see for ourselves that the **block chain is independent and more stable than anything else**.

Never before in the history of this planet, have individuals and has the **normal citizen been given a choice** in by what financial system, what monetary policy, what level of transparency they like to be governed by, what system they like to live in and with. Now we have that choice. Let us choose wisely. **Let us not be cattle raised by unfaithful stewards any longer.**

For the first time, we have that choice to vote with our feet (i.e. our money).

---

[93] [http://bitcoinmagazine.com/10702/economists-hate-bitcoin/]

Sapere aude!

Have courage:
to use your own faculties,
to make use of your own reason.
Have the courage to be your own bank.

7 Short resource list

7.1 Link List (related websites, news, tools)

[www.bitcoin.org]
Website of the Bitcoin foundation

[https://en.bitcoin.it/wiki/Main_Page]
Bitcoin Wiki maintained by the community.

[https://blockchain.info/]
Bitcoin block chain explorer

[http://ripplebot.com]
Lets you look up Ripple addresses, see their transactions, offers made and cancelled, trust lines, limits, etc.

[http://coinmarketcap.com/]
Lists most known crypto-currencies sorted by their market share and price and offers graphs concerning their current and past exchange rate.

[www.howtobuybitcoins.info]
Link list of places / exchanges to buy Bitcoins (and other currencies) for individual countries (worldwide). Lists also payment and transfer methods

[http://bitcoincharts.com/]
Provides financial and technical data related to the Bitcoin network.

[www.coindesk.com]
News provider on prices and information on Bitcoin and other digital currencies.

[cointelegraph.com]
News provider, analysis, review on bitcoin and other digital currencies.

[https://www.coingecko.com/en]
CoinGecko is a crypto-currency ranking chart app that ranks digital currencies by developer activity, community, and liquidity.

[https://coinist.co]
Offers expert and user ratings of currencies, protocols and assets. Crypto-currency "Rating Agency"

7.2 Password generators

use at your own risk

[http://passwordsgenerator.net/]

[https://identitysafe.norton.com/password-generator]

[https://www.grc.com/passwords.htm]

7.3 Books on the problems with the old system

Books that are dealing with the inherent issues of the legacy system: fractional reserve, central banking, government administered, politically controlled, not stable, not secure, economic exclusion and self-made macro-economic disasters.

Miyazaki, Hirokazu: **Arbitraging Japan: dreams of capitalism at the end of finance**, University of California Press, Berkley, 2013, ISBN 978-0-520-27347-4

James Rickards: **Currency Wars**: The Making of the Next Global Crisis (Aug 28, 2012)

James Rickards: **The Death of Money**: The Coming Collapse of the International Monetary System (Apr 8, 2014)

Sara Eisen: **Currencies After the Crash**: The Uncertain Future of the Global Paper-Based Currency System (Oct 23, 2012)

Matthew A. Hinde: **The Money Myth** - How the Current Financial System Really Works: and Why We Need to Change It. (Jan 6, 2014)

Arthur Cohn: **Kann das Geld abgeschafft werden?** (Feb 15, 2014)

Michael Goodwin, David Bach: **Economix: How Our Economy Works** (and Doesn't Work), in Words and Pictures (Sep 1, 2012)

Mann, Ian, **Hacking the human**: Social Engineering Techniques And Security Countermeasures, Gower Publishing, 2008, ISBN: 978-0-566-08773-8

Eric M. Jackson, **The PayPal Wars**: Battles with eBay, the Media, the Mafia, and the Rest of Planet Earth, 2004, ISBN: 0974670103

Fred L. Block, **The Origins of International Economic Disorder**: A Study of United States International Monetary Policy from World War II to the Present, 1978, ISBN: 0520037294

C. Bresciani-Turroni, **The Economics of Inflation**, Augustus M. Kelley, New York, 1968 reprint of 1937 edition

7.4 Books on Virtual Currencies and Bitcoin as an alternative

Testimony of Andreas M. Antonopoulos before: THE STANDING SENATE COMMITTEE ON BANKING, TRADE AND COMMERCE, OTTAWA, Wednesday, October 8, 2014, Evidence Transcript Document: BANC 51627, 1610- 1

link: http://www.parl.gc.ca/SenCommitteeBusiness/CommitteeTranscrip ts.aspx?parl=41&ses=2&Language=E&comm_id=1003 [41st Parliament, 2nd Session (October 16, 2013 - Present)]

Bryan Keen: **BITCOIN GUIDE FOR BEGINNERS**: Unmasking the currency that has created millionaires out of few dollars investment (Jul 25, 2014)

Daniel Kerscher: **Handbuch der digitalen Währungen**: Bitcoin, Litecoin und 150 weitere Kryptowährungen im Überblick (Augt 26, 2014)

Alex Nkenchor Uwajeh: **Bitcoin and Digital Currency for Beginners**: The Basic Little Guide (Jun 4, 2014)

Dr. Raju Oak and Charmaine Oak: Virtual Currencies - From Secrecy to Safety: **The Evolving Landscape in the Bitcoin Era** (Aug 29, 2014)

Edward Castronova: **Wildcat Currency**: How the Virtual Money Revolution Is Transforming the Economy (Jun 3, 2014)

Jose Pagliery: **Bitcoin: And the Future of Money** (Sep 1, 2014)

Pierre Noizat: **Bitcoin, monnaie libre** (Sep 9, 2012)

Andreas M. Antonopoulos: **Mastering Bitcoin**: Unlocking digital crypto-currencies (Nov 25, 2014)

Philippe Herlin: **La révolution du bitcoin** et des monnaies complémentaires August 19, 2014

Daniel Forrester, Mark Solomon: **Bitcoin Explained**: Today's Complete Guide to Tomorrow's Currency (Mar 12, 2014)

Chris Clark: **Bitcoin Internals**: A Technical Guide to Bitcoin (Jun 15, 2013)

Michael Caughey: Bitcoin Step by Step (Nov 10, 2013)

Sam Patterson: **Bitcoin Beginner**: A Step By Step Guide To Buying, Selling And Investing In Bitcoins (Dec 4, 2013)

Mike Fishbein: Bitcoin 101: The **Ultimate Guide to Bitcoin** for Beginners: Bitcoin Market, Crypto-currency and Bitcoin Basics (May 28, 2014)

Brian Kelly, **The Bitcoin Big Bang**: How Alternative Currencies Are About to Change the World, 2014

7.5 Videos relating to Bitcoin

The real value of bitcoin and crypto currency technology - **Bitcoin Properly**:
http://www.youtube.com/watch?v=YIVAluSL9SU#t=355

Video of the testimony of Andreas M. **Antonopoulos** before the Senate of Canada about Bitcoin (Oct 8, ENG)
http://www.youtube.com/watch?v=xUNGFZDO8mM

Bitcoin Crypto-currency **Crash Course** with Andreas Antonopoulos - Jefferson Club Dinner Meetup:
http://www.youtube.com/watch?v=JP9-lAYngi4

What is Bitcoin? And Why Should I Care? - Jeremy Allaire @ MIT Bitcoin Club:
http://www.youtube.com/watch?v=ZloserjZNfM

Bitcoin vs. Political Power: The Crypto-currency Revolution - **Stefan Molyneux** at TNW Conference:
http://www.youtube.com/watch?v=joITmEr4SjY

'Bitcoin steals power from both banks & gangsters'
http://www.youtube.com/watch?v=as_3Pp_yGq4

Everything You Need to Know About Bitcoin
http://www.youtube.com/watch?v=SNssKmeXrGs

8 A list of gateways / exchanges

8.1 General Information

Beware: Data provided might be outdated / incomplete.
In any case do double check addresses and fees with the respective website and the gateways banking partner.

Including gateways in this list is not an endorsement or any comment on their trustworthiness.

Time of compilation: October 2014

Online resources listing major currencies and exchanges with a description of their details:

Coinst: [https://coinist.co/ripple/gateways]

Coinmarketcap: [http://coinmarketcap.com/currencies/views/all/]

Coingecko: [https://www.coingecko.com/en]

8.2 List of selected Bitcoin exchanges (in alphabetical order)

ANX [https://anxpro.com/] [https://anxbtc.com]

Bitfinex [https://www.bitfinex.com/]

BitSource [https://bitsource.org/]

Bitstamp [https://www.bitstamp.net]

BTC-e [https://btc-e.com/]

BTC China [https://www.btcchina.com/]

CampBX [https://campbx.com]

Kraken [https://www.kraken.com/]

Localbitcoins.com [https://localbitcoins.com]

SnapSwap [https://snapswap.eu/]

8.3 List of selected Bitcoin exchanges (with details)

Bitstamp (http://www.bitstamp.net/)

   Currencies traded: XBT, USD

   Contact: info@bitstamp.net

Free SEPA deposit and withdrawal, minimun transfer of 10 €, Astropay

0.5% XBT commission

OKCoin CN (https://www.okcoin.cn/)

   Currencies traded: XBT CNY LTC

   Contact: service@okcoin.com / QQ:800045125

0% trade fees

OKCoin US (https://www.okcoin.com/)

   Currencies traded: XBT CNY LTC USD

   Contact: service@okcoin.com

XBT Trade 0.2-0.1% LTC Trade 0.2-0.1% USD Withdrawal 0.1%

BTC China (https://vip. BTCchina.com/)

Currencies traded: XBT, CNY

Contact: business@BTCchina.com

CNY Withdrawal: 0.38%,
withdrawal amount less than 200 CNY cost 2 CNY fee.

Bitfinex (https://www.bitfinex.com/)

Currencies traded: LTC XBT USD DRK

Contact: support@bitfinex.com

Lake BTC (https://lakebtc.com/)

Currencies traded: BTC, USD, CNY

Contact: LakeBTC@gmail.com / help@LakeBTC.com

0.2% commission, reduced fee for reteweeting

BTC-E (https://btc-e.com/)

Currencies traded: XBT USD EUR GBP RUR CNH LTC NMC
...

0.5% commission USD / RUR

ITBIT (https://www.itbit.com/)

Currencies traded: BTC USD EUR SGD

Contact: info@itbit.com

0.5% commission, decreasing scale on large volumes

UrduBit (https://www.urdubit.com)

Currencies traded: PKR, XBT

Trade 0.75% commission, PKR Deposit / Withdrawal 1%

Coniage (https://coinage.ph/)

Currencies traded: XBT, PHP

Currencies traded: support@coinage.ph

0.25% transaction fee

8.4 List of Ripple gateways (in alphabetical order)

A list of Ripple Gateways is available from the Ripple website at [https://support.ripplelabs.com/hc/en-us/articles/202847686-Gateway-Information].

Bitso [https://bitso.com]

Bitstamp [http://www.bitstamp.net/]

btc2ripple [https://btc2ripple.com/]

Coinex [https://www.coinex.co.nz/]

Gold Bullion International [http://www.bullioninternational.com/]

Justcoin [https://justcoin.com/] [closes down 11.11.2014, reopens 24.11.2014]

Kraken / Payward [www.kraken.com]

Panama Bitcoins [http://ptycoin.com/ripple]

Payroutes [https://payroutes.com/]

Rippex [https://rippex.net]

Ripple China [https://trade.ripplechina.net/]

Ripple Fox [https://ripplefox.com/]

Ripple Singapore [https://www.ripplesingapore.com/]

Ripple Trade Japan [http://rippletrade.jp/]

Ripple Union [https://rippleunion.com/]

RippleCN [http://www.ripplecn.com/]

Ripplewise [https://www.ripplewise.com/]

Ripplex [https://ripplex.co.jp]

SnapSwap [https://snapswap.eu/]

The Rock [https://www.therocktrading.com/]

Tokyo JPY Issuer [http://tokyojpy.com/]

Wisepass [https://wisepass.com/]

8.5 Ripple gateway list in order of jurisdiction

Brazil   Rippex [https://rippex.net]

Canada, KitchenerRipple Union [https://rippleunion.com/]

China   RippleCN [http://www.ripplecn.com/]

China, Shanghai   Ripple Fox [https://ripplefox.com/]

China, Shanghai   Ripple China [https://trade.ripplechina.net/]

EEA / Norway   Justcoin [https://justcoin.com/]

EU / Latvia   SnapSwap [https://snapswap.eu/]

EU / Malta   The Rock [https://www.therocktrading.com/]

EU / Slovenia   Ripplewise [https://www.ripplewise.com/]

EU / UK / Slovenia   Bitstamp [http://www.bitstamp.net/]

EU / UK, London   Wisepass [https://wisepass.com/]

Israel   Payroutes [https://payroutes.com/]

Japan, Hamamatsu   Ripple Trade Japan [http://rippletrade.jp/]

Japan, Tokyo   Ripplex [https://ripplex.co.jp]

Japan, Tokyo   Tokyo JPY Issuer [http://tokyojpy.com/]

Mexico   Bitso [https://bitso.com]

New Zealand   Coinex [https://www.coinex.co.nz/]

Panama   btc2ripple [https://btc2ripple.com/]

Panama   Panama Bitcoins [http://ptycoin.com/ripple]

Singapore   Ripple Singapore
[https://www.ripplesingapore.com/]

USA   Gold Bullion International
[http://www.bullioninternational.com/]

USA   Kraken / Payward [www.kraken.com]

USA   SnapSwap [https://www.snapswap.us/]

8.6 Ripple gateways (with details)

Selected gateways are presented below in the following format:

Gateway / Exchange Name (website)

Ripple name: ~

Public Address:

Currencies issued / traded:

Contact:

(withdrawal, transfer fees and limitations)

(Special information)

Ripple network transactions are not charged (but a tiny fraction is taken to prevent spamming)

5 biggest exchanges (showing a market share on [ripplecharts.com]) first, then sorted alphabetically:

Bitstamp (http://www.bitstamp.net/)

 Ripple Name: ~Bitstamp

 Public Address: rvYAfWj5gh67oV6fW32ZzP3Aw4Eubs59B

 Currencies issued: BTC, USD

 Contact: info@bitstamp.net

Free SEPA deposit and withdrawal, minimun transfer of 10 €,

Astropay

International bank transfer (not SEPA): 0.09% fee, minimum fee is $15.00
(minimum withdrawal is $50.00)

Special: 2-factor authentication available, location: Slovenia / UK, cooperating bank: www.rbinternational.com (Raiffeisen Bank)

RippleCN (http://www.ripplecn.com/)

   Ripple Name: ~RippleCN

   Public Address: rnuF96W4SZoCJmbHYBFoJZpR8eCaxNvekK

   Currencies issued: BTC, CNY

   Contact via QQ: 2849481838

Withdrawal fee: 0.3%, at least 2 CNY maximum 300 CNY

Paypal withdrawal, Chinese Bank withdrawal

Ripple China (https://trade.ripplechina.net/)

   Ripple Name: ~RippleChina

   Public Address:
razqQKzJRdB4UxFPWf5NEpEG3WMkmwgcXA

   Currencies issued: BTC, CNY, LTC

   Contact: goodx@ripplechina.net / maggie@ripplechina.net

0.6% fee, on Alipay / Tenpay or bank platform.

Shanghai, Hangzhou and Shenzhen

Ripple Trade Japan (http://rippletrade.jp/)

   Ripple Name: ~RippleTradeJapan

   Public Address: rMAz5ZnK73nyNUL4foAvaxdreczCkG3vA6

   Currencies issued: JPY

   Contact: info@rippletrade.jp

Deposit Fee for Japan Post or other Japanese Bank transfer: 1% (minimum 100JPY)

Japanese Bank withdrawal fee: 1% plus
(for amount < JPY 30 000 / > JPY 30 000): JPY 258 / 165, except Sumishin SBI Bank: JPY 51

SnapSwap (https://snapswap.eu/)

   Ripple Name: ~SnapSwap

   Public Address: rMwjYedjc7qqtKYVLiAccJSmCwih4LnE2q

   Currencies issued: USD, EUR

   Contact: support@snapswap.com

Location: Latvia,
Deposit fee: 0.99% + €0.30 per transaction

Withdrawal fee: 0.99% + €1.00 per transaction

(SmartyCash rechargeable Prepaid Visa card,
without international payment fee, with 5% bonus on purchases,
except cash, promotion period)

btc2ripple (https://btc2ripple.com/)

    Ripple Name: ~btc2ripple

    Public Address: rMwjYedjc7qqtKYVLiAccJSmCwih4LnE2q

    Currencies issued: BTC

btc2 ripple is operated by snapswap

in alphabetical order from here

Bitso (https://bitso.com)

    Ripple Name: ~bitso

    Public Address: rG6FZ31hDHN1K5Dkbma3PSB5uVCuVVRzfn

    Currencies issued: BTC, MXN, USD

    Contact: contact form at website

Coinex (https://www.coinex.co.nz/)

    Ripple Name: ~Coinex

    Public Address: rsP3mgGb2tcYUrxiLFiHJiQXhsziegtwBc

    Stellar Address: gs9HHU3pmkKBuvykhNm6xiK1JKrput9i3K

    Currencies issued: BTC, USD, NZD, AUD

    Contact: support@coinex.co.nz

Location New Zealand, Fiat deposit and withdrawal limit: $50,000 per month,

Withdrawal via Ripple /Stellar / Bitcoin / Bank: 0.20 / 0.50 / 0.50 / 1.00% per transaction

International Bank withdrawal: 25 $, cooperating bank: www.bnz.co.nz

Gold Bullion International (http://www.bullioninternational.com/)

    Ripple Name: ~GBI

    Public Address: rrh7rf1gV2pXAoqA8oYbpHd8TKv5ZQeo67

    Currencies issued: XAU

    Contact: info@bullioninternational.com

Justcoin (https://justcoin.com/)

    Ripple Name: ~justcoin

    Public Address: rJHygWcTLVpSXkowott6kzgZU6viQSVYM1

    Currencies issued: BTC, LTC, XRP, EUR, USD, NOK, STR

    Contact: support@justcoin.com

SEPA/ SWIFT deposit: NOK 20 / 50 NOK

Norwegian domestic transfer free

SEPA / SWIFT withdrawal: 30 / 60 NOK

Daily withdrawal limit: 80 000 NOK

Special: One time password/2-factor authentication available, mCash, location: Norway, cooperating bank: www.dnb.no

Update: Justcoin suspended trade on 29.10.2014 and announced to close on 11.11.2014,
Update #2 announced on 18.11.2014 to reopen under new management of the ANX exchange on 24 .11.2014

Kraken / Payward (www.kraken.com)

Ripple Name: **planning to become a Ripple Gateway**, no ETA at present,
(you will be given Ripple / Bitcoin / Stellar adresses to deposit and withdraw)

Currencies traded in the exchange: BTC/XBT, USD, EUR, XVN, LTC, XRP, NMC, XDG, STR

Contact: https://support.kraken.com

Crypto fee schedule until 0.1%, Fiat fee until: 0.35%
depending on trade volume of last the 30 days

Payroutes (https://payroutes.com/)

Ripple Name: ~PayRoutes

Public Address: rNPRNzBB92BVpAhhZr4iXDTveCgV5Pofm9

Currencies issued: USD, ILS, BTC, LTC, NMC, PPC

Contact: support@payroutes.com / info@PayRoutes.com

Deposit fees: 5 NIS, withdrawal fees: 40 NIS, EgoPay,

deposit / withdrawal fees: NIS 0.50 + 2.50% / 0, transfer fees: 0.20%

Monthly withdrawal limit: NIS 30 000

Panama Bitcoins (http://ptycoin.com/ripple)

  Ripple Name: ~ptycoin

  Public Address: rBadiLisPCyqeyRA1ufVLv5qgVRenP2Zyc

  Currencies issued: USD, PAB, BTC, LTC, DRK

  Contact: info@ptycoin.com / exchange@ptycoin.com /
info@panamabitcoins.com

BTC deposit to Ripple account after 3 confirmations,
or personal a "BTC embassy meeting" also accepting cash at meeting,
USD deposit via ACH no fees from Pptycoin, SnapSwap USD
and Bitstamp USD at 3% deposit fee

Rippex (https://rippex.net)

  Ripple Name: ~rippex

  Public Address: rfNZPxoZ5Uaamdp339U9dCLWz2T73nZJZH

  Currencies issued: BRL

Location: Brasil, Must be citizen with Brazilian bank account to
withdraw,

deposit / withdraw limit per day: R$ 10.000,00,
deposit / withdraw fee: R$ 1,50 + 0,5% / R$ 1,50 + 1,5%,
transfer fee: 0.3%, TED / DOC chargeback: R$ 20

Ripple Fox (https://ripplefox.com/)

    Public Address: rKiCet8SdvWxPXnAgYarFUXMh1zCPz432Y

    Currencies issued: STR, FMM, CNY

    Contact: support@ripplefox.com

Withdrawal/redemption fees: 0.1% (charging at least 2CNY)

Deposit over Alipay / Taobao, QQ group: 389185252

Ripple Singapore (https://www.ripplesingapore.com/)

    Ripple Name: ~RippleSingapore

    Public Address: r9Dr5xwkeLegBeXq6ujinjSBLQzQ1zQGjH

    Currencies issued: SGD, USD, XAG, XAU, XBT

    Contact: Support@ripplesingapore.com

Free Gold/Silver/Platinum Bullion storage over Silver Bullion Pte Ltd,
Location: Singapore, cooperating bank: www.ocbc.com

No Capital Gains Tax due on bullion held in Singapore

No deposit fees, Withdrawal fees (Giro/FAST/MEPS): S$ 5/10/25

Ripple Union (https://rippleunion.com/)

    Ripple Name: ~RippleUnion

    Public Address: r3ADD8kXSUKHd6zTCKfnKT3zV9EZHjzp1S

    Currencies issued: CAD

Contact: help@rippleunion.com / singpolyma@singpolyma.net

deposit or withdraw max. CAD 150 via Interac e-Transfer
to your Ripple Wallet (fee: 2 CAD)

Ripplewise (https://www.ripplewise.com/)

    Ripple Name: ~ripplewise

    Public Address: ra98sfbmYvVF9AQWKS3sjDBBNwQE85k2pE

    Currencies issued: BTC, USD

    Contact: support@ripplewise.com

Ripplex (https://ripplex.co.jp)

    Ripple Name: ~ripplex-llp

    Public Address: r9ZFPSb1TFdnJwbTMYHvVwFK1bQPUCVNfJ

    Currencies issued: JPY

    Contact: contact@ripplex.co.jp

Deposit / withdrawal fee: 1.08% (during promotion 0%),
Flat fee for Japanese bank withdrawal: 540 JPY

The Rock (https://www.therocktrading.com/)

    Ripple Name: ~therock

    Public Address: rLEsXccBGNR3UPuPu2hUXPjziKC3qKSBun

    Currencies issued: BTC, LTC, NMC, PPC, DOGE, EUR, USD

Contact: info@therocktrading.com

SEPA withdrawal <1000 / >1000 €: 1 / 4 €

EGOpay, OKpay, stock exchange included

location: Malta, cooperating bank: www.bov.com

Tokyo JPY Issuer (http://tokyojpy.com/)

Ripple Name: ~tokyojpy

Public Address: r94s8px6kSw1uZ1MV98dhSRTvc6VMPoPcN

Currencies issued: JPY

Contact: contact form at website

Wisepass (https://wisepass.com/)

Ripple Name: ~Wisepass

Public Address: rPDXxSZcuVL3ZWoyU82bcde3zwvmShkRyF

Currencies issued: USD, BRL, BTC, CAD, CHF, DKK, DOG, EUR, FTC, GBP, JPY, LTC, NOK, SEK

Contact: hello@wisepass.com

Free inbound, Transfer fee: 0.025%

8.7 Banks that use the Ripple Network for international transfers

The banks listend below have joined the Ripple Network and are at present offerening (or might be offering in the future): foreign currency or asset exchange and transfer or other advanced services at rates below the traditonal banks.

Fidor Bank AG Germany (www.fidor.de)

Sandstr. 33
80335 München
Deutschland

info@fidor.de

Bankleitzahl: 700 222 00

BIC: FDDODEMMXXX

"Social banking": offering different boni and incentives
facebook sign up, third party offers with cash back, etc., Prepaid Smart MasterCard,
Full account legitimization (with standard bank account number and IBAN)
only through German PostIdent and registered address in Germany

Cross River Bank (www.crossriverbank.com)

885 Teaneck Road
Teaneck, NJ 07666
United States

info@crossriverbank.com

CBW Bank (www.cbwbank.com)

109 E Main St
Weir, KS 66781

United States

info@cbwbank.com

8.8 Stellar gateways

(detailed description see Ripple gateways above)

Coinex (https://www.coinex.co.nz - based out of New Zealand)

Ripplefox (https://www.ripplefox.com - based out of China)

Justcoin (https://justcoin.com/)

8.9 (Other) Stellar Exchanges

(currently trading the STR/BTC pair)

Bx.in.th (https://www.bx.in.th - based out of Thailand)

BTC38 (http://en.btc38.com - based out of China)

Ybex (https://ybex.co -based in China)

AllCoin (https://www.allcoin.com/)

Stellarix (https://stellarix.pw/#)

Poloniex (https://poloniex.com/exchange/btc_str)

ANXPRO (https://anxpro.com)

Crypto-Trade (https://crypto-trade.com/)

Kraken (https://www.kraken.com)

9 Glossary

51% attack - A situation where the majority of nodes (measured in computing power) release intentionally false data.

Account - Bank account, online account or wallet

Alt-coin - Other alternative digital currencies and protocols

AML - Anti-Money Laundering requirements

Bank - A market place for traditional money and debt. Charging fees for services provided.

Bitcoin (protocol) - Software-based online payment system as first introduced in 2009, distributed (peer to peer) and open source

Bitcoin white paper - A paper authored by Satoshi Nakamoto in November 2008: 'Bitcoin: A Peer-to-Peer Electronic Cash System'.

BitPay - A payment processor for Bitcoins, which works with merchants, enabling them to take Bitcoins as payment

BitStamp - A Bitcoin exchange, located in Slovenia

Block chain - A list of validated blocks, each linking to its predecessor all the way to first block

BTC (digital currency) - A unit of the Bitcoin decentralized virtual currency / Crypto-currency (a more internationally standardise abbreviation XBT was proposed)

Checksum - A checksum is a cross sum or sum of digits for the purpose of detecting errors in longer strings of characters

Client - A desktop, mobile or online program connecting the user to the Bitcoin network, forwarding transactions. (may also include wallet function)

Colored coins - A proposed add-on enabling Bitcoin users to mark a Bitcoin as a share of stock, or a physical asset.

Confirmation - Once a transaction is included in a block, it has "one confirmation".

Convert - Immediate sell or buy order at market rate

Crypto-currency - A Crypto-currency is a medium of exchange using cryptography to secure the transactions and to control the creation of new units.

Cryptography - Codes and ciphers that are the basis for the mathematical problems used to verify and secure Bitcoin transactions

DDoS - A distributed denial of service attack

Deflation - The reduction of prices in an economy over time. When people expect falling prices they stop spending and hoard money. This can have negative, negatively reinforcing effects on an economy.

Destination tag - A number added behind a public address to distinguish user's funds from others accounted for under the same address. Comparable to the practice of using c/o with postal addresses. E.g. "?dt=12356"

Difficulty - Determining how much computation power is needed to verify a block of transactions, it is variable depending on the Bitcoin price.

Exchange - A market that changes one currency into another applying an exchange rate. Charging fees for services.

Fee (Bitcoin) - An excess amount included in each transaction as a network fee or additional reward to the miner

Fiat - Traditional national or regional currencies

FinCEN - The Financial Crimes Enforcement Network, an agency within the US Treasury Department.

Gateway - (In Ripple) a market that can be integrated into the trade client (integrated exchange).

Genesis block - The first block in the block chain, used to initialize the crypto-currency

Inflation - The value of money drops over time, causing prices for goods to increase. The result is reduced purchasing power.

KYC - Know Your Client rules force financial institutions (and exchanges) to require proper identification of users (opposite of trust your customer and presumption of innocence)

Ledger - Consensus between the peers verifies the transaction of digital currency units in a common ledger (the block chain)

Liquidity - The ability to buy and sell an asset easily, without high price fluctuation to occur during the transaction

mBTC - 1 thousandth of a Bitcoin (0.001 BTC)

Microtransaction - Paying a tiny amount for an asset or service, primarily online.

Mining - Creation of new units within a Crypto-currency protocol (if not pre-mined), transfer verification, backbone of the payment system

Mixing service - A service that mixes your Bitcoins with someone else's (also known as a tumbler) potentially used for money laundering

Network - A connection of peers that propagates transactions

Node - A computer connected to the Bitcoin network using a client that relays transactions to other nodes

Open source - Software or protocol code being made publically available, so it can be reviewed

Order book - Orders to buy and sell a fixed amount at a fixed priced are placed in a database at an exchange. A graph can be drawn to visualise the market

OTC exchange - Over the counter exchange, an exchange in which traders make deals with each other directly, rather than relying on a central exchange to mediate between them.

Paper wallet - A printed sheet containing a public Bitcoin address and its corresponding private keys. If safely stored no backup is required on any computer or online. The data on the paper can always be re-imported and used to access funds.

Peer to peer - Peer-to-peer (P2P) computing distributes tasks or work loads between different computers (peers). All peers are equal (equipotent participants).

Private key - A password required so send Bitcoins from one public address to another

Public key - Is the alpha-numeric address of a users funds on the block chain (different protocol = different address)

Pump and dump - Inflating the value of a financial asset that has been produced or acquired cheaply, using aggressive publicity and often misleading statements.

QR code - A two-dimensional black and white picture (dot matrix) representing a sequence of data. QR codes are designed to be scanned by cameras, frequently used to encode website addresses, e-mails, and other public addresses

Ripple (protocol) -Deflation based pre-mined payment protocol operated by Ripple Labs Inc.

SEPA - Single Euro Payments Area established through Directive 2007/64/EC of the European Parliament and of the Council of 13 November 2007 on payment services in the internal market

SHA-256 - The cryptographic function used as the basis for Bitcoin's proof of work system

Stellar (protocol) - Inflation based payment protocol operated by the Stellar Development Foundation (a non-profit organization)

STR (digital currency) - A unit of the Stellar decentralized virtual currency / Crypto-currency

Transaction - A transfer of Bitcoins from one address to another

Volatility - The measurement of price movements over time for a traded financial asset

Wallet - A place (client, program) used to send Bitcoin and manage your keys. Online or locally installed repositories that can store keys and can be used to transfer digital currencies (USB wallet, paper wallet, memory wallet, hardware wallet).

XRP (digital currency) – The native unit of the Ripple decentralized virtual currency / crypto-currency / payment protocol